RISING SUN BLINKING

A young boy's memoirs of the
Japanese occupation of the
Philippines

José María Lacambra

iUniverse, Inc.
New York   Bloomington

RISING SUN BLINKING
A young boy's memoirs of the Japanese occupation of the Philippines

iUniverse books may be ordered through booksellers or by contacting:

iUniverse
1663 Liberty Drive
Bloomington, IN 47403
www.iuniverse.com
1-800-Authors (1-800-288-4677)

Because of the dynamic nature of the Internet, any Web addresses or
links contained in this book may have changed since publication and may
no longer be valid. The views expressed in this work are solely those of
the author and do not necessarily reflect the views of the publisher, and
the publisher hereby disclaims any responsibility for them.

Cover © Sinag Tala Publishers, Manila, 1994

ISBN: 978-1-4502-0326-5 (sc)
ISBN: 978-1-4502-0327-2 (ebook)

Printed in the United States of America

iUniverse rev. date: 03/05/2010

This is a story of two young boys who
tweaked the Emperor's nose during
World War II, made him blink, and lived to tell.

The adventures and rites of passage
here described were drawn from a diary
the author kept during those war years.

Though time and memory may have altered
a few events, all the characters are from real life.

This story is dedicated to youth, its
dreams, its ardors, and its sometimes
uncompromising courage.

J.M.L.
Winter Park, FL.
March, 1995

Contents

Contents

1. RUDE AWAKENINGS

Iru's angry bark turned to a pained yelp. I knew it wasn't the Colonel's horse this time around; the terrier couldn't possibly have reached the town square to nip at the stallion's heels, as he'd done every afternoon since the Japanese invaded our island. Turning the corner, I saw the white fox terrier limping toward me, hind legs dragging. Blood gushed from a deep gash in his back every time he breathed.

Stooped over, less than twenty yards away, a Japanese soldier was wiping his bayonet on the grass. Straightening up suddenly, he sheathed his weapon and walked away, without even a backward glance. There was something vaguely familiar about his stooped shoulders and loping gait, or maybe it was just the way he carried himself, I wasn't sure. But then, suddenly, the moment he turned his head to cross the street, I recognized him.

It was Uyeki!

I was stunned. His uniform had thrown me off. Odd though it seemed at first, it suddenly dawned on me that his being Japanese only made it natural and inevitable.

"You bastard!" cried out something raw and livid inside me, but not a sound emerged from my throat. A deep-seated instinct warned me that Uyeki could just as easily turn around and use his bayonet on me. I just stood there, in helpless, bewildered rage, watching him disappear in the gathering shadows of Calle Real.

Iru's brown eyes were looking up at me, as if pleading to make things alright again. I held his gaze until he became too blurred to see. He was whimpering more softly now, eyes starting to glaze over. I had never seen anything die before and was overcome by a feeling of helplessness, watching his life ebb away in my arms.

My mind went blank when Iru died that evening. I was only twelve, and too young for that kind of pain. I gasped for meaning, trying to fathom why anyone would take away life so wantonly. Mom and Dad tried to comfort me but their sympathy blew over me like dry wind on parched earth. Only the old believe that grief is bearable.

"He was such a friendly sort!" I tried to describe Uyeki to my kid brother, Luis, that night in bed. "He was the kind'a guy who'd get upset when someone in class got rowdy, can you believe it?"

"He was a lot older than any of you, wasn't he?" queried Luis.

"Yeah, but you couldn't tell it by just looking at him. You know how Orientals are, ageless kind'a. It was his height, I think, and those round, wire-rimmed glasses of his that gave his age away, a little, anyway."

"You used to say he was so shy," puzzled Luis. "Wonder what made him change so."

"Shy but smart. Tops at anything he tried. Except English; he was lousy at English. Couldn't pronounce his el's if his life depended on it. Jesus Jimenez used to kid him about it. 'Once-in-brue-moon Uyeki' he used to call him. He hated it.

"Was he good at other subjects too?" Luis pursued.

"He was a whiz at Math. You should'a seen him whip out those answers with that abacus of his! And he played the harmonica pretty well, too! He hypnotized us all with all those Deanna Durbin and Carmen Miranda and Betty Grable songs he'd play!"

"I bet he was good at drawing, too, wasn't he," remarked Luis. "Orientals are great at drawing."

"That was his favorite subject! You should'a seen him dipping that horsehair brush of his in India ink and then spreading the black goop around on silk paper. Before you knew it, you'd be staring at some misty mountain scene from his homeland, or somewhere exotic. Uyeki was a one-man act, no but's or if's!"

"Sure sounds like a different guy to me. Kind'a like that Jekyll and Hyde fellow in the movies," commented Luis in the dark, under his bed sheets.

"I can't figure it out myself. He was such a shy, gentle guy, always eager to belong, be one of the crowd. A little confused, sometimes. About his Jap-ness, I mean. Especially right there before the war. We used to tease him about how the Yanks were gonna beat the stuffings out of the Japs if they didn't start behavin'. He just sat there, smiling that inscrutable smile of his."

"I think you just done broke the code!" remarked Luis shrewdly; he was almost ten but already far keener than his years. "And that concentration camp they slapped them into when the war broke out probably didn't help any, either. Bet'cha he was a spy, all along."

"Come to think of it, I bet he was, too! He's probably one of a handful of Japs in this whole Occupation Army who speaks Visayâ. Makes him a dead ringer for this 'Kempitai' thing."

"What's that, Kempitai?" asked Luis.

"You know, it's that outfit they call 'Military Intelligence.' Bunch of guys snooping around the population, picking up tidbits here and there, roughing people up if they don't toe the line. Spook works, that sort of thing."

We were still trying to fathom Uyeki, late into the night. But Iru was dead and no amount of psychoanalysis was going to bring him back. His loss had left me with a numbness that would linger for a long time. I could see that Lobo, the German shepherd, also missed him, the way he'd sniff around the house after him, simpering like a soul in pain.

As the days went by, my grief gave way, almost imperceptibly, to a quiet, smoldering anger, with deep tones and dark shades that only revenge would soothe. An insane urge had gurgled up into consciousness and was beginning to take shape in my mind, crowding out all other thoughts: Iru's death had to be avenged. Nothing else would do. I would wage my own war against Uyeki and his evil Empire!

Like a skittish octopus, the Japanese Empire had spread its tentacles across the islands, after the last American strongholds of Bataan and Corregidor had fallen. By April of 1942, they had landed on our island, deep in the heart of the Philippine Archipelago. After combing the hills around the hamlet where we'd been holed up since Pearl Harbor, they hustled us back to town at gunpoint.

My eyes smarted with the sweet, acrid smell of burnt molasses, the day we drove back to Iloilo. The city with the lilting name lay in ruins. In a scorched-earth frenzy, the local Constabulary had set whole sections of town to the torch. Stunned, the returning population searched aimlessly among the rubble, dazed by the wandering smoke and devastation around them.

Miraculously, our house survived the holocaust. Its massive, four-foot thick coquina walls had survived the skirmish, mocking fate the way they had taunted time. The old Colonial residence had been my happy home. It had enough alcoves and antechambers and secret recesses to satisfy any child's wildest hide-and-seek fantasies. I still remember the scroll-molded stairway sweeping grandly up to a reception hall, where countless introductions had been made and appointments kept, when Dad was Spanish Consul in town.

"Race you!" I challenged Luis when we got to the landing.

"You're on!" he answered, sensing, but not greatly minding, the false start.

The outcome was never in doubt. I out slid him down the stairway's balustrade and was first to touch the now-shiny right nipple of the bronze Nyad that stood pert guard at the bottom of the scrolled sweep; that was our secret home base.

"No fair! You cheated!

"I beat you fair and square!"

I knew I hadn't, of course, but rationalized that firstborns have their privileges...and little humilities to bear, because, deep down, I knew that my kid brother's heart had more gold in it than mine. He must have been five when Mom found him frantically blowing air under the door of a closet where I'd accidentally locked myself in, thinking I was suffocating inside.

But we were too close in years to let the odd tender moment interfere with the roughhousing. The Yaya doled out punishment with great abandon, but the nanny's ear-boxing and pinching merely brought on the giggles. Dad had ordered boxing gloves from Sears & Roebuck to cut down on nosebleeds and black eyes. It worked for a while but the rivalry remained, undiminished.

Even during the hallowed quiet of Dad's siesta hour, we'd be at it, snapping wet towels at each other, or crashing toy cars against each other, or engaging in paper airplane fly-offs, littering the garden below. I'll never forget the afternoon we were laughing so hard, shaking talcum powder and splashing water at each other, when Dad stormed into the bedroom to settle disrupted siesta accounts. His slipping on the pasty talcum goop, trying to extract us from under the beds, didn't help matters any.

The first day home from the hills, I could already sense that something had changed. War seemed to have dulled the grin of sunshine, stilling the laughter that once echoed along the halls. Even the art Deco rattan furniture, once the rage, just sat there now, looking like some dowager's dated heirlooms, in a living room whose interleaved Lauan and Kamagong hardwood floorboards seemed to have lost their sheen. The ceiling fans no longer paddled the humid air, nor did the ancient brass fittings spew water anymore; utilities had been cut and would remain interrupted for the duration. We'd have to make do with kerosene lamps and rainwater, from here on out.

But if only the luster had dimmed in ours, other homes had suffered a grimmer fate. There was nothing left of the Davies' residence, next door. Only a heap of rubble now lay where the regal mansion had once stood. Dad, Luis and I ambled over to see if we could salvage anything from our friends' home. Splintered timber lay all about, helter-skelter, as if a tornado had touched down on it. My heart sank as I surveyed the devastation around us.

"What an unholy mess!" I commented, heartbroken.

"Look at these molten glass nodules!" exclaimed Luis, picking up one of them. "Must'a been that huge chandelier that used to hang over the hall."

"Gee, remember all those parties?" I reminisced, refusing to believe the end of an era. I could almost feel the ghosts of black-tied gentlemen huddling importantly around that very hall, savoring Cognac-dipped Havanas and talking over their snifters about foreign contracts and diplomatic appointments, while their wives sat nearby, dressed fit to kill, playing Mah-Jong.

Something shone dully under my feet. Picking it up, I recognized the tiny, solitary TV screen, all smudged and unfulfilled.

"Turn it on," I remembered begging Lawson Davies, after the ice cream and the cupcakes. "See if it's started already."

The tow-haired Scot would shuffle over to the veneered, cathedral-shaped TV set that sat in this very corner of the living room over whose ashes I now stood. The cyclopic screen would light up obediently enough, when turned on, but then merely hissed its white noise at us. It'd be years before the first TV program would be aired in the Islands. Not to be bested, the Jimenez, next door, had an air conditioner which, for lack of Freon, never worked either. But that was alright because in that outpost of waning Empire, one-upmanship was still a game played in deadly earnest.

Stepping among the rubble, Dad leaned over and picked up a blob of half-molten silver.

"Ashes of memories," he said almost inaudibly, turning the remains of the golf trophy in his hands. "I'll never forget that tournament," he said wistfully. "We beat Gene Sarasen that day, John and I did."

Despite the hurdle of language, Dad and Mr. Davies had been golf and tennis partners and best of friends, probably because they both had the luxury of being quiet, like strong men sometimes do. Their businesses had intertwined; Dad directed a Spanish Conglomerate's sugar operations while Mr. Davies, a shipping tycoon, exported the sugar sacks all over the world. They both spoke in monosyllables, like Gary Cooper used to do in the movies. It must have been their economy of expression and shared love of golf, tennis and hunting that threw the Basque and the Scot into each other's company.

"Look at this!" remarked Luis, stooping over to pick up a tarnished silver spoon. "We must be standing where the dining room used to be!"

How well I remembered it, those many years on! I could almost taste the dark, gamy meat at the big hunter's party, the time Dad and Mr. Davies brought down a wild *jabalí* boar in the mountains, nearby. I'll never forget the improbable grin etched on the beast's apple-stuffed mouth when the servants brought it out of the kitchen, groaning under the weight of the laden heavy silver tray.

"*Salúd!*" Mrs. Davies had toasted tentatively in the middle of dinner, raising a giddy cup. Lawson and I giggled at his mother's expansive attempts at Spanish, inspired by a little red wine. Mrs. Davies was a lovely Scottish lady who, probably much to her distress, was often reminded of her faint resemblance to the Queen, later called 'Mum.'

"Wonder what's happened to the Davies," I asked Dad. "Lawson said they were staying put while everyone else was leaving town after that first Japanese bombing."

"That's what John told me they'd do," confirmed Dad. "I'm afraid he put more stock in that 'Prince of Wales' Man-O-War than the Japanese did. Thought a single solitary British battleship was enough to discourage Japanese adventures in the China Sea."

I could tell from his furrowed brow that he was troubled. "Sure hope they got away from under this mess," he said, looking at the splintered shambles around us.

"Let's go back home," he said finally, after we tired of shuffling through the rubble. He was still holding on to the gnarled golf trophy. "We'll pay them a visit in concentration camp. Surely that's where they are."

2. FIRST IMPRESSIONS

Jesus Jimenez was standing at the bottom of the stairs, watching Luis and me slide-race down the balustrade, yet another time. He had heard through the grapevine that we were back in town.

"That was another of his false starts, Luis! I saw it!" he cried in his high-pitched, squeaky voice, trying to fan a sibling rivalry that needed little outside encouragement.

"Hey, how ya doin'!" we greeted with feigned indifference. We hadn't seen each other since the exodus from town, four-month earlier.

Jesus Jimenez, Lawson Davies and I were about the same age and best of friends. Jesus' dad was a Bank president but the covey of Yayas that that afforded was never enough to keep the hyperactive Jesus under control, as he was growing up. Fr. Badillo, our language teacher whom we nicknamed Budul, referred to him as 'a wilderness crying in a voice,' a description that always brought to mind the RCA mutt, inanely howling into its master's gramophone speaker.

"What kept you guys so long? Where've you been, anyway?" he asked in a tumble of words. Lost above a finely-chiseled nose, his brown eyes peered out keenly from sunken sockets, like accidents in search for a place to happen. I noticed he was still using Petrolatum Vaseline to control the unruly cowlick that crowned his broad forehead.

"Igbarás," I answered. "Neat little town in the hills, about thirty miles west of here. We got to ride horses and carabaos and all sorts of neat things. I even got thrown out of bed one night, during a big earthquake. It was so huge it cracked the wall of the town's old Colonial church! How about you guys, where'd you go?"

"Holed up in our Otón beach house. Great swimming but bo-o-ring! The Japs ended up landing right near there. Talk about excitement! They shooed us out of there in a big hurry. Told Dad he had to reopen the Bank right away."

"They chased us out of the hills too, after shooting up the local Constabulary," interjected Luis. "Mean-looking bunch, these Japs, aren't they?"

"Tell me about it!" said Jesus. You could always tell when he was warming up to some tall tale. "I saw a bunch of soldiers standing at attention around the kiosk in Plaza Libertad, as I rode by there on my bike the other day. Some Officer was blessing them out while this poor grunt stood next to him, his right arm stuck out in front of him. Pretty soon the Officer stops barking, turns around, whips out this huge sword and, whoosh! lops off this poor bastard's hand with a single stroke. The guy never even flinched!"

Jesus paused for effect, before adding: "I almost threw up!"

"What did this guy do, anyway?" I asked, a little incredulous.

"Stole a chicken, or somethin', someone said. Can you believe it?"

"Rawtha ghastly!" remarked Luis, sharing my disbelief. I could tell he still had Lawson in his mind.

"Did'ja hear from him at all?" asked Jesus, picking up on the imitation. "Someone told Dad their house took a direct hit from a Jap artillery shell."

"Something hit it, alright," I said. "That house sure looked a mess! We're going to concentration camp to visit him one of these days. He'll tell us all about it. Wanna come along?"

"Sure! Poor guy. Must be tough being cooped up in concentration camp all this time," commented Jesus. "I bet Lawson's already figured out a way to dig his way out of there, though. He could probably use a shovel, or something, don't you think?"

"A shovel!" I mocked. "Small wonder he calls you 'Barmy'. I hate to think what they'd lop off of me if they caught me smuggling a shovel in there!"

"Hey, you guys wanna see something funny?" Jesus said, changing the subject. "Come on, follow me. I'll show you" he shouted, running out the door without waiting for us.

13

I always worried about Jesus' harebrained schemes; something always seemed to go awry with them, like the time he suggested we sling-shoot a beehive off of a tree in his backyard. They didn't have enough Mentholatum ointment at the San Pablo Hospital to soothe all those bee sting lumps on our heads and shoulders. Or the green *guavas* in their orchard he was always tempting us with. God, I hated the Castor Oil we'd have to take afterwards! Dad swore by the laxative.

Skipping across the town square, we headed for the Masonic Temple, where Luis and I finally caught up with Jesus Jimenez. The Japanese had commandeered the large granite building for their Military Government offices. As we walked past it, the Japanese sentry standing guard in front of the main entrance started barking orders at us.

"*Koko e kite!*" he shouted at us irately, beckoning us toward him. The short, squat soldier was gripping a huge bayonet-affixed rifle in one hand, motioning us toward him with the other. Approaching him with great trepidation, I noticed his steel dentures gleaming through an evil smirk. He smelled faintly of stale sweat. It was my first face-to-face confrontation with the enemy, and I was a little scared.

Being the tallest of the three, he motioned me to lower my head, as if in reverence to him. "You bow!" he ordered gruffly. Unhappy with the initial results, he grabbed me by the hair with his free hand and yanked my head down to belt level. The rifle's butt next to my face discouraged any thought of resistance or escape.

Finally satisfied, he swiveled me around brusquely and laid a boot on my rear before dealing with Luis and Jesus. The lesson in Japanese civility was humiliating.

"You knew he was going to do that, didn't you," I snapped at Jesus, after we'd left the premises.

"That was some long bayonet, wasn't it?" he said, trying to skirt the subject. "Dad says Napoleon used to swear by that weapon. Said the tool's so useful you can do almost anything with it, except sit on it." He giggled.

"Did they commandeer your car too?" he continued.

"They took our Hudson the day we drove back from Otón. Borrowed our radios, too. Said they'd return them after they snipped off the shortwave band off of them. That's so we can't listen to the war news, you know. Pretty sneaky bunch, huh?"

"Yeah, our Desoto's gone too," Luis answered. "So's Dad's .32 pistol. You know, the one with the pretty mother-of-pearl handle. They took those away the first day back from Igbarás."

"They took our radios too," I added. "But just before they did, we heard the Brits licked the Germans in some tank battle in Egypt. So they're not such hot stuff, after all."

"Too bad," commented Jesus in a resigned tone. "They'll come around, though. Just you watch."

15

For some odd reason, Jesus had always favored the Germans. I think it was just to be ornery, like those rocks that stick out of a river sometimes, just to buck the current, trying to change its course. He loved talking about Panzers and Stukas and 88's. He and Lawson almost came to fisticuffs once, when he said the Brits were 'a bunch of ninnies,' right after the Dunkirk disaster. That touched a raw nerve with Lawson.

"How about San Agustin?" I asked Jesus. "When do they reopen?"

"I hope they remain closed permanently," he responded. "I don't think I can take much more of Fr. Budul's knuckle raps."

After a thoughtful pause, he added: "Dad's threatening to send us to that nuns' school on General Hughes Street." He pronounced it 'Hah-ges' like his dad used to, believing that every vowel deserved the decency of a syllable, like in Spanish.

"That's just ducky!" remarked Luis disgustedly. "I hope he doesn't give Dad any ideas." Girls were not his cup of tea and being cooped up with a bunch of them, however temporarily, wasn't his idea of fun. "Even Budul sounds better to me!"

"I guess you're right," agreed Jesus. "But, boy, I hate going back to those chick peas!"

The Augustinian friars who ran our Boys' School had some rather medieval notions about education. 'Thwack 'em hard and burry 'em with homework', that seemed to be their motto. Fr. Budul was pretty enthusiastic about both teaching approaches.

"Should be a bullwhip instead of that crucifix sitting on his desk," muttered Jesus. "More appropriate."

Fr. Budul must have read his thoughts because he always had him under his sights. He'd make 'you barbarian,' as he used to call Jesus Jimenez, kneel on a pile of chickpeas purposely strewn in a front corner of the classroom, every time Jesus stepped out of line, which was often. When the period ended, Budul would shuffle over to Jesus, knuckle-rap him on the head, clout his ears and yank him up by his sideburns. The class bristled in righteous, but subdued indignation.

Jesus quickly caught us up on the more noteworthy happenings in town during our absence. Several of our classmates had become casualties during the first Japanese bombing raid. Zoilo Apellaniz was killed outright, while his brother Jaime was seriously wounded, trying to protect him. Noli Atayde was still walking around with a .50-caliber bullet lodged next to one of his kidneys, apparently not much the worse for wear.

"That Noli's like crab grass, aint he?" Jesus commented.

"The Botica Boie drug store's reopened but they're plumb out of ice cream sodas and Cokes and Chicklets. Even Batman comics, can you believe it! Dad says there's gonna be no more Gillette blades till the war's over. My sisters are moanin' about running out of Odor-O-No deodorant and those furry little mouse-like gadgets they call Tampax. I think the worst thing of all is they're all out of Feenamint.

You know what that means, don't you? Back to Castor Oil. Ugh!"

"I noticed they've boarded up the Roxy and the Palace theaters," I remarked. "No more Hoot Gibson and Tim McCoy movies for a while, I guess."

"Yup, and no more new records, either. Actually, I'm getting pretty sick and tired of 'Chattanooga Choo Choo' and "In the Mood' and 'Bugle Boy,'" complained Jesus. "That beat up old gramophone of ours is scratching my Tommy Dorsey's and Benny Goodman's pretty bad."

It sounded as if time had stopped and had decided to take a step backward to take a jaundiced look at things. I suspected something like this would happen the morning I walked in on Mom and Dad half a year earlier, while they listened to the news about Pearl Harbor on the radio. I was almost eleven then but could already sense that things were about to unravel.

And yet, despite the end of running water and Big Band records, life slithered back to normal, grudgingly. The help, which had abandoned ship the day war broke out, started trickling back, one by one, soon after we returned from the hills. Consolación, our inappropriately named Yaya, was the first to turn up. She'd nannied for Luis and me when we were kids, and had now graduated to the position of maid.

I was glad to see Angel return. I loved watching the crusty old Chef force Brandy down capons' and turkeys' gullets a few hours before slaughtering them. "Gives them character," he'd mumble through his half-chewed beetle nut cud.

Next back were Eusebio and Juan, the two male servants enigmatically called 'boys,' despite their getting on in years. They had doubled up as trackers whenever Luis and I would give Consolación the slip.

Attired in her plaid sarong, Alíng Andáng, the washer woman, sailed into the house some days later, preceded by her conical, foul-smelling stogie, clamped between her random teeth. Occasionally, Alíng would smoke cigarettes, only backwards; ember side carefully nestled in the hollow of her tongue so the ashes wouldn't fall on her ironing. When nature beckoned, she'd simply straddle the narrow rain gutter bordering the downstairs patio, pull the front and back of her loose sarong away from her, and relieve herself, smiling blissfully as she went.

Juan Sumalakay was the last to turn up. Short of five feet tall, the 'old midget,' as Jesus Jimenez used to call him, had been head chauffeur in Dad's Company, for years. He drove an ancient World War I Ford truck, hauling sugar sacks from plantations to warehouses. Looking very much like a displaced Brontosaurus, the ancient conveyance now sat stolidly on its solid rubber tires in the murky depths of the enormous downstairs patio.

The Japanese had scorned the relic, a slight which, at once, pleased and hurt Juan's feelings. Short of gas, the old truck never went anywhere now, but Juan still pampered it anyway, polishing its brass lamplights and fondling its choke and throttle knobs. Occasionally, he'd honk its sensuous goose horn. A cherubic smile would wash over his furrowed face as the flatulent noise bounced around the disturbed patio walls, sounding very much like someone with a cold had blown a huge nose.

The family chauffeur and the gardener never came back. Cirilo must have rightly sensed that the Desoto was now gone, and Tiburcio, the gardener, had had his fill of Luis and me, having to pick up after our needle-nosed paper fighters and blunt bombers, while also trying to revive his sickly *gumamela* hibiscus bushes, which had always smelled suspiciously of urine ammonia. Besides, he must have reasoned, Victory plots would soon replace his flower beds and Bermuda grass lawn, anyway, and farming was definitely beneath his talents.

3.   A BROTHER GIVEN

The compound was bristling with guards. The dour-looking soldiers appeared unhappy; they'd been trained to fight the enemy, not coddle it. Curtly, the Corporal of the Guard ushered us into the Commandant's office.

"Why you want to visit," inquired the Captain sourly. It was only nine o'clock but the spreading sweat stain in his shirt's underarms betrayed his discomfort in the muggy tropical morning.

"We'd like to visit friends," Dad answered in his deep, carrying voice. The authority in it made the Officer tone down his surliness, but only a notch.

"You have half hour," he grunted. "No gifts except toilet articles. We have to inspect all packages."

They let us in after the formalities. The interns milled around the dirt grounds looking bedraggled and ill kempt, as if they hadn't had enough time to pack up any belongings before being whisked off to concentration camp. Our presence was soon noticed. The inquisitive stare of all those deep-set, haunted eyes made me feel ill at ease. Several of the inmates recognized us. Shrubsole, a shy, retiring English classmate of mine, ambled slowly toward us, as if to conserve energy.

"How ya doin' Peter?" I asked awkwardly, after fishing for, and not finding, something more appropriate to say. He'd always been a loner in school and had few, if any real friends.

Shrubsole looked at me from behind sunken sockets. He looked haggard.

"O.K., I guess," he responded listlessly. Then, after a brief pause, he asked: "How come you guys are not in here with the rest of us, anyway?"

"Spain's neutral," I answered, almost apologetically. "We're lucky that way, I guess." The conversation was getting more awkward by the minute. "How're they treating you guys?"

"Could do with a little more food some days."

"What are they feeding you guys, anyway" asked Jesus Jimenez, sounding very much as if he were getting ready to sort things out with the Camp Commandant.

"A bowl of gruel a day."

"Listen," I whispered in his ear, "we aren't supposed to bring you anything except soap and stuff like that, but if you open your hand, I'll slip you something you'll like."

He looked puzzled at first, but did as asked. I'd been saving my last stick of bubble gum for some more memorable occasion but Shrubsole's haunted eyes told me this was it.

"Thanks!" he said, without even looking down at the gift. "Boy, I can even smell it!" he added, eyes suddenly coming alive. It struck me odd that he could smell anything, let alone a stick of stale bubble gum, but then I thought probably hunger sharpened one's senses.

"O.K.," I answered. "Now you gotta tell us where the Davies hang around in this place."

His eyes widened in surprise. "They're not here," he answered almost inaudibly. "Didn't you hear? They were killed during the invasion. Jap artillery shell slammed into their house. Direct hit. They found Mr. and Mrs. Davies' bodies in the basement, but no sign of Lawson. Not even a trace. Shell must'a disintegrated him, or something. Poor bloke!"

I was stunned. The enormity of the news left me shuddering, as if I myself had been straddled by the salvo. A numbing pain sank slowly into deepest consciousness, where, as if in slow motion, it suddenly exploded into a thousand painful shards that scythed away at childhood memories of friendship and camaraderie. Helplessly, I groped for answers. First Iru and now this! I felt as if slowly drawn into some whirlpool whose dark, animate waters were starting to lap around me.

"How'd you find out about the Davies?" asked Luis.

"Uyeki. The bugger was smiling when he told me," responded Shrubsole sullenly. "Uyeki and I were classmates, you know?"

"How long are they keeping you guys in here?" asked Jesus Jimenez.

"Believe they're taking us to Santo Tomás in Manila next week," said Shrubsole. "Some big University there they've turned into a concentration camp."

"They'll probably treat you better there," I said lamely, trying to comfort him. "You take care of yourself, Peter," I said, resting a hand on his shoulder. As we parted, I remembered how he used to shy away every time any lapse of honor threatened in class. I was sure he'd keep out of trouble in Manila.

We visited other friends in camp that morning. The looks of quiet resignation in their drawn, joyless faces depressed me. Their todays must have been so awful you could tell their tomorrows were figuring greatly in their thoughts. About the only good news in that dispirited camp was that their meager diet had caused old Fr. McCarthy's diabetes to slip into remission. He'd been the ageing Chemistry teacher at San Agustin, who'd shuffle along in the lonely evening of a teacher's life, longing for a well-earned retirement, now cruelly disrupted by war.

Several weeks after the Camp visit, Dad and I biked over to the Sagrado Corazón Girls' School. The Augustinian friars were taking their sweet time reopening our Boy's School, and Dad was growing increasingly impatient, what with Luis and me getting constantly underfoot around the house. Besides, Mr. Jimenez had told him he was sending his own boys to the Girls' School, to mark time. That, of course, sealed our fate.

"*Hola, paisano!*" greeted the Mother Superior cheerfully, when we were shown into her office. Like Mom and Dad, she too hailed from Navarra, the old Basque Kingdom in northern Spain. They'd known each other for years and had been close friends.

The lively exchange of war news soon turned to small talk. During a lull in the conversation, Sister Felicidad suddenly turned earnest.

"I need your advice," she said, lowering her voice. "Promise that what you're about to hear remains within these four walls."

"Promise," Dad and I answered in unison. People always trusted Dad. Something about his makeup seemed to compel confidence. Friends would bare their inmost secrets to him, name him trustee to their fortunes, and judge in their family squabbles. If I had to describe him with a single word, I'd use 'honorable.' He was honest to a fault and, like the straight arrow he was, just as predictable. I only heard him swear once in my life, and the English cuss word he used went unnoticed; he had mispronounced it.

"You know, I presume, that the Davies died during the invasion," the nun was saying. After we nodded assent, she continued: "What you may probably not know is that their son, Lawson, survived."

"No!" I cried out in disbelief, overwhelmed by a great sense of joy and relief. In the short space of only a few weeks, I had learned about his death, and now that he was alive! "Where is he? How'd he survive? Is he O.K.?" I asked, stumbling over something in me that kept leaping for joy.

25

"Their chauffeur found Lawson moaning in the basement right after the shelling. His parents were killed outright but a fallen beam saved Lawson's life. He was in shock, both legs broken and all cut up with lacerations. The chauffeur suspected that Hospital San Pablo had already been overrun, so he thought of us. He knew that all of us St. Vincent nuns are trained for school and hospital work. So he braved the shells and drove Lawson out here at midnight. How's that for loyalty!"

"Renews one's faith in the human spirit, doesn't it?" agreed Dad. He, too, was visibly moved.

"How's Lawson? Where's he now?" I asked impatiently.

"He's mending quite nicely," answered the Sister. "He's already walking around. But that's the problem," she said, turning to Dad. "We can't keep him here indefinitely. Parents are already pressing us to reopen the school and we can't keep Lawson under wraps once classes start. Too much time has gone by since they interned the others. They've already sent the rest of them to Manila," she reflected. "I'm afraid of Japanese reprisals on my Community for harboring a prisoner of war all these many months."

Dad mulled over the nun's predicament for what felt like a long time. And then, almost abruptly, he reached a surprising decision.

"I'll take Lawson into my family," he said. "I can't do otherwise. I'll adopt him as my son. When the war's over, he can return to his family in Scotland, if he so chooses."

Sister Felicidad was just as stunned as I by the unexpected suggestion. She seemed reluctant to show any premature sense of relief.

"How do you propose to hide him from the Japanese?" she asked warily. "It'll be a while before the Americans return, you know. The long wait could spell danger for all of us."

"Never mind the details. What's right is right," Dad persisted. "It's the least I can do for a good friend. I realize there are a few loose ends in my plan right now but I'll sort it all out. Besides," he added, "living with us will help Lawson overcome his sense of loss. He needs to be with boys his age to help him get over it. He was good friends with my sons, you know."

The nun nodded but remained skeptical, her eyes riveted on Dad as if waiting for some clinching revelation.

Puzzling over the quandary for a few more moments, Dad finally arrived at a stunning solution.

"Until I'm relieved from my post, I remain Spain's Consul in this island. I can draw up a legal instrument of adoption that'll make Lawson a Bona Fide citizen of Spain. We're a neutral country, so that should keep him out of concentration camps. It'll also provide him a safe haven in our home."

"The timing is a little tricky," he continued, "but, under the circumstances, there are no options other than turning him in. You and I know we're not going to surrender Lawson to the Japanese. It'll all work out. Don't fret over it," he reassured the nun.

27

Sister Felicidad finally allowed herself to smile. It was a clever ruse.

"You are as good and noble as the land that bore you," she said, tears of pride and gratitude welling up under her soft brown eyes. But for the impropriety of the gesture, I believe she would have hugged him.

Embarrassed by her gushing, Dad brought up the question about our starting school at the Sagrado Corazon until our own Boy's School reopened.

"But of course! Other families are doing the same. It'll take a few weeks before we open, though. I'll let you know."

As we walked out of her office, I asked Sister Felicidad if I could see Lawson.

"He's in the infirmary right now, resting. You'll see him soon enough," she answered, equably.

I was a little disappointed, but thought I shouldn't be greedy. Lawson was not only alive and well; he was going to become my brother to boot! It felt as if a grin of sunshine had suddenly broken through some murky windowpane inside me, splattering everything with sunlight. A brother! And this one chosen!

"*Vaya con Dios, paisano,*" said the Sister in parting, her voice breaking slightly as she clasped Dad's hand with both of hers.

Everyone at home was elated when Dad broke the news about Lawson's survival and his decision to bring him home as soon as he could draw up the proper adoption and citizenship papers. He'd have to get the seal of approval from the Spanish Embassy in Manila, but that was just a formality. Meanwhile, he swore the household to discretion until the papers were properly legalized.

"You have a new brother," he told Luis and me at dinner that evening. "He will be one of the family from now on. He'll even bear our name. He still grieves the loss of his parents, but time heals all sorrows. When the time comes, he may choose to return to his own flesh and blood in Scotland. He has two older brothers there, as you know. But meanwhile, you must be kind and gentle with him. He's one of us now."

After dark one evening, not long after, Lawson came home with Dad. Having a new brother felt like Christmas and Epiphany, all rolled into one. The reunion was moving, the moment of meeting poignant as a dart. He was paler than I remembered, thinner too, to the point of gauntness. But he was the same old Lawson, his clear blue eyes and tow-haired fairness betraying his Viking origins. He even had the same old freckles Jesus Jimenez used to tease him about, blaming his mother for sneezing a mouthful of cocoa on him, when he was born.

We hugged in silence, a little bashful and self-conscious at first. And then small words started to wander out between us. It wasn't long before we got down to the easy conversation of youth, when words, like thoughts, are free and untrammeled. Before long, Luis and I had Lawson in stitches, with stories about our mountain exploits in Igbarás. The private language soon followed.

"Zinker tinkle der ningle?" I queried him.

"Pip!" he answered enigmatically, with a perfectly straight face.

Luis and I giggled knowingly. Nobody, not even we, knew what the words really meant. They just sounded funny, that's all. Consolación, had overheard the exchange and looked distressed. The old Yaya could still not abide the gibberish, hoping we'd outgrown it by now.

Jesus Jimenez had started the mysterious language years earlier. "Keedle!" he piped up one day, trying to describe Carceller's adenoidal, Elmer Fuddish kind of look. "He's got a 'keedle' face!" He didn't have to explain it further. It just fit. And that was the beginning of our secret nonsense language.

"How about "Fulmi?" Lawson had proposed, the time we were searching for a handle for bald men like Mr. Obeso. The word evoked the full moon which his magnificent, billiard-ball pate resembled, and was, therefore, incorporated, by unanimous vote.

Luis himself had come up with a winner when we were hunting for some whimsical name for thin-necked, weak-chinned people, like Silvestre Apellaniz, who worked at a bookstore downtown.

"Gumphy!" he had proposed, without even blinking his big blue eyes. And 'Gumphy' he was rechristened, despite the fact that others were already calling him *'tiro rapido,'* or 'quick draw,' sarcastically alluding to his painfully slow elocution.

Our Yayas hated the gibberish because they could never fathom the nonsense language, which sometimes sounded perfectly naughty, but really wasn't. Like *"Dorken schlaben in einen Ausfahrten,"* which never failed to annoy Hans Weber, who suspected we were poking fun at his beloved German, which we, of course, were.

Ives Partier didn't like it, either, when we'd sidle up to him, droop our eyebrows and curl our lips, like constipated Frenchmen do, uttering dumb Gallicisms like *"Tu-tu fornu?"* which must have sounded perfectly awful to his sensitive Alsatian ears, the way he grimaced. The infernal language lived on, as if imbued with a life of its own. It now came back unbidden, fresh with thoughts of happier days.

"You know you're no longer English," I said to Lawson. "You're Spanish like us now."

"I was never English, dummy! I'm Scottish"

"No more, you're not!" Luis intervened.

I could never figure out why Lawson would get so upset whenever I referred to him as English. "It's your mother tongue, ain't it?" I'd ask, perplexed.

"So?" he'd counter huffily. "You speak Visayâ but aren't Filipino!" That settled ruffled Scottish feathers, for the time being, anyway.

But he knew he'd have to learn Spanish now. He'd just turned eleven, an unself-conscious age when foreign languages come easily. It didn't take him long to break out in Spanish. The trilled r's and the Castilian lisp always brought on the giggles. Jesus Jimenez took charge of his greening in the vernacular, which, of course, very quickly landed us all in trouble at the dinner table.

One thing he did get used to quickly enough was Angel's cooking, rich in garlic and onion seasoning. I don't think he missed his Yorkshire puddings much, nor had tea and crumpets been at the top of his list. Much to everyone's delight, Lawson quickly got used to our Spanish ways.

The first few nights after he came home, I'd watch him slip quietly out of bed and walk out on the upstairs patio by himself. From my bed, I could see him standing there with hunched, hopeless shoulders, elbows resting on the balustrade, shedding silent tears of loss. I could only surmise that it was the din of conscience, brutally reminding him that some survive only because others die. It broke my heart that I could do nothing for him in those private moments of grief.

I told Mom and Dad about it.

"He has moved from innocence to pain," Mom tried to explain. "And now, orphan-hood makes him feel limp and empty. Try to be sweet to him."

"Time heals all wounds," Dad added. "Just be yourselves with him and everything'll soon be alright."

4. SCHOOL OF KNOCKS

The long school break came to an abrupt end one sultry summer morning, in mid 1942, when the bells of Sagrado Corazón started tolling once again. Going back to books after half a year's vacation was traumatic enough, but having to attend a girls' school was devastating. We twitched restlessly under unfamiliar rules of feminine conduct, but seldom skipped a chance to test the nuns' patience, nor relented in our open rebellion against the coeducational order. Awareness of our transient status in the girls' school only compounded the mischief.

Jesus Jimenez was in his element. His very own sisters were so mortified by the havoc he managed to wreak inside the precinct that they started disclaiming him as a brother. Mayhem was, of course, second nature with Jesus. Since nothing brought it on quicker than boredom, Sor Caridad, the Religion teacher, ended up bearing the brunt of his unmitigated delinquency.

"O.K.," he proposed one day, only a week into classes. "Today we pull the syncopated humming stunt." While Sister Caridad was droning on about Purgatory, Jesus Jimenez started humming in his corner of the classroom. Just as she thought she'd tracked the source of the disturbance, someone else picked up the droning elsewhere until, pretty soon, the whole class was humming with abandon. Sister Caridad came pretty close to the verge of apoplexy, that day.

"Now, how's this for a humdinger," Jesus proposed a few days later. "Today, after class, everyone goes out and catches a fly and keeps it in an empty matchbox. In Religion class tomorrow, we take it out, carefully stick a little piece of paper up its rear end and, when I give you guys the signal, we all set them loose at the same time. You got that?"

Sor Caridad was in the middle of a lecture on Original Sin when the bespangled insects were turned loose. As soon as she spotted the droning peace flags buzzing overhead, the nun went unstable. Awash with laughter, the class watched her chase after them, muttering in damaged agitation as she ran from one end of the classroom to the other, swatting at the flies.

Nuns love skits and recitals. It didn't take much of an excuse to get one of their mystical celebrations going, but when the feast of the Assumption rolled around, they really went overboard. We'd watch them, morosely, as they scurried around the school grounds, giggling with excitement, draping banners and streamers, and strewing spangles and confetti all over the place. The girls, too, turned giggly nervous, in anticipation of their skits and poem-reading contests.

Morning Mass at the chapel kicked off the festivities. Fr. Pampliega, the grumpy Chaplain whom we'd nicknamed

'Pampols,' was waxing eloquent during the homily when Jesus Jimenez, who was sitting next to me, proudly broke wind. The report was so sonorous and irreverent that the whole congregation, except for the nuns, broke out in giggles. Offended by the toot, the Sisters started casting withering glances in our direction, threatening to subtract us bodily from the congregation. Their reproving looks only redoubled our mirth until, finally, Jesus and I had to leave the chapel, convulsed with chortles.

Inquisition proceedings started soon after, trying to get to the bottom of the turmoil that had visited the girls' school, ever since classes started. Rumor had it that though they'd reached a consensus, they lacked sufficient incriminating evidence to warrant expulsion. Surely, a single person could not generate all that havoc, they must have conjectured. And so, the only action item taken was a redoubling of vigilance to pounce on the suspect at his very next misdemeanor, Bank President's son or not.

Only Lawson came out smelling like a rose, in those unsettled days. Being their adoptive son, he could do no wrong by the nuns; they had, after all, nursed him back to life. But their favoritism only embarrassed him. They'd flutter around him during recess, cornet headwear getting in each other's way as they vied for his attention. Lawson wasn't even Roman Catholic but, strange to say, the nuns respected his earnest Presbyterian convictions. Religious fairplay may have been the unspoken price exacted by Dad for having relieved them of their burden. I'll never know.

"You have to take piano lessons with me," I overheard Sister Imelda, the music teacher, chirping at Lawson one day. Lawson not only turned a deaf ear to the invitation but joined Jesus, Luis and me that evening when we snuck up under the Music room's pane-less windows to lob a couple of lit firecrackers into it, disrupting some girl's sol-fa exercises inside. The ensuing shrieks sounded sweeter in our ears than had her earnest falsettos.

"Dad says the nuns are begging the friars to reopen San Agustin as quickly as possible," said Jesus one day at recess. "They can't stand the heat anymore," he sniggered.

"Whose heat?" asked Lawson. "Seems to me you set most of those fires yourself, you delinquent! Now you'll have Budul's chick peas to worry about. You didn't know a good thing while you had it, you pimple head!"

"I've got more battle calluses in a single knee than you've got freckles in your dorky face. I can take Budul on any time. You just worry about yourself," Jesus sniffed huffily.

San Agustin opened its doors soon enough. Dad had alerted the friars to Lawson's change of name and nationality, and nobody gave it a second thought. Most of his old classmates believed he was Irish, anyway, and was, as such, just another neutral citizen. Those who knew better were happy to join in the conspiracy.

"It's like a game of hide-and-seek," commented Lawson. "The Japs are 'it' all the time, and don't even know it!"

"Hope they don't ever wise up," I commented.

Despite the more severe discipline awaiting us there, we were delighted to be back in our own Boy's school. Its fortress-like walls beckoned dubious welcome, their wrought iron-barred windows discouraging all thought of late entry or furtive exit. Surrounding its acres of playing fields was a maze of acacia-lined avenues, where white-robed Augustinian friars could be seen taking their late afternoon constitutional, mumbling Vespers in jaded boredom.

Row upon row of wooden desks lined the dank classrooms, their sloping, inkwell-pierced tops bearing stains of countless spills and lacerations of past generations that had managed to muddle through in their confused road to learning. Competing for attention with the wooden crucifix above the teacher's desk were lithographs of Millet's "Man with the Hoe" and "The Gleaners," with somber social messages that escaped us.

Although the majority of the students were Filipino, the Spanish friars lectured in English, using American textbooks. Like the radios before them, the Japanese had retrieved all textbooks, sanitizing them by pasting over illustrations bearing anything American in them. The first thing we did, on retrieving the books, was to peel the pasted paper right off them. Most of the time, we'd discover harmless illustrations of the Empire State building, or the Golden Gate bridge, or some cornfield in Iowa. But I hit pay dirt on scavenging in my Algebra book, when I uncovered a wrinkled picture of a B-l7 soaring grandly in the vacant California sky.

"What a great name, 'Flying Fortress'!" I commented to Lawson, showing him my trove. We hadn't the slightest clue that we'd one day be on the receiving end of that airplane's formidable bomb load. But we loved airplanes. I remember an article on the Lightning P-38 warplane, published in one of the last Saturday Evening Post issues we received just before the war broke out. The sleek, three-bodied fighter was the fastest warplane of the day. Every kid in school admired its graceful lines and sleek aerodynamics.

Using the article's pictures for blueprints, I spent several weeks carving a model of a P-38 out of crate wood. Carving and pasting the little air inlets on the sides of the twin fuselages was tough and tedious work, but the really tricky business was sawing off the nose cones of the two booms in order to insert the propellers behind them. Then, after sanding down the separate pieces and gluing them together, I coated the work of art with aluminum paint and propped it up on a wooden stand.

"It's a thing of beauty, ain't it?" I glowed over it with Luis and Lawson.

"Yup," agreed Luis. "It's a good thing the Japs didn't walk in here while you were building an enemy airplane model."

"Yeah, I guess you're right," I said. "Can't be too careful with these guys." Grudgingly, I took the model and hid it in the basement.

I wasn't the only one who worried about the Japanese. Father Budul looked distraught the first few days of school. They had changed the goalposts on him, forcing him to teach Japanese instead of Latin. It was bad enough that this new, barbaric language lacked periphrastics and subjunctives and supines with which to torment hapless students. Now, he had to struggle with a bewildering variety of hieroglyphics.

Japanese writing was baffling enough but having to teach oriental tunes was pushing Japanese culture one step too far. As if all this weren't trouble enough, Jesus Jimenez, Budul's nemesis, would occasionally slip Visayan barbarisms into the Japanese lyrics. His classmates' ensuing howls, greatly distressed Fr. Budul.

"These songs are downright cacophonic!" muttered Jesus Jimenez defensively, when reprimanded. He was always picking up these big words from his older brothers. This one, he explained to us later, came from combining 'caca' and 'phonic.' He seldom cracked a smile when he said something outrageous like that, so we never quite knew whether to believe him or not.

It didn't take long to notice Uyeki's absence in school. It was several months since he had killed Iru, but memories of that afternoon lingered, vivid and un-forgiven. We soon confirmed our suspicion that despite his young age - he was all of eighteen now - he'd been commissioned an Officer in the Kempitai, the dread Intelligence Branch of the Japanese occupation forces. His knowledge of the local population, its dialect and customs, made the assignment inevitable.

Every now and then we'd see him strutting about town with brisk importance, a .45 strapped to his belt and an evil, gold-toothed grin permanently set in what used to be an expression-less face. The transformation was complete. Luis, Lawson and I would cross over to the opposite side of the street whenever we'd see him approaching. Noticing the ploy one day, he beckoned us over to him and started berating me about the 'bad old days' in school, reminding me of the way we'd mistreated him.

Squeezed in puzzled thought behind his wire-rimmed granny glasses, Uyeki's eyes turned suddenly quizzical when they focused on Lawson's sandy hair and undeniably Saxon storm of freckles.

"Who he?" he asked gruffly, pointing at Lawson. My heart drummed against my throat. I gulped hard, sensing that Lawson's moment of truth was at hand. It was time to put to the test all those endless hours of practice, when we'd tried to mask his Scottish brogue under a thick layer of Spanish idioms. Unfortunately, there had been more mirth than learning in those outrageous sessions.

"He's my kid brother," I stuttered in a confined voice, trying to sound halfway plausible. Lawson had been one grade behind Uyeki and me in school, and I was hoping that they had never actually met in the school grounds. Just as I thought he'd swallowed my story, Uyeki resumed his questioning.

"*Anataa no otooto desu ka*?" he asked suspiciously, not quite buying the brother story. I stared at him blankly, pretending I hadn't understood the question.

"He your brother? Why he got brue eyes," he pursued in a harsh tone.

Lawson had remained silent during the interchange, looking on with mounting concern, trying to maintain an aloofness he hardly felt.

"It runs in the family, see?" I answered in desperation, pointing at Luis who was standing nearby, gawking at the perplexed oriental with his own big blue eyes.

"*Ohayoo Gozaimasu!*" greeted Luis with an inappropriate 'Good Morning', it already being late afternoon.

A lingering doubt persisted in Uyeki's shifty eyes. Then, quite unexpectedly, Uyeki turned on me. Angered at not having figured it all out by himself, without outside help, he gripped me by the scruff of the neck with a powerful hand, lifted me up with a violent jerk and delivered me a swift, jackbooted kick in the seat of the pants. Flinging me aside disgustedly, he stormed off in a clatter of boots, muttering Japanese expletives, as he went.

"This perishing Jap's a regular bugger, ain't he," commented Lawson, as soon as we were out of earshot.

"A regular pip!" I agreed, borrowing one of his favorite expressions. "This guy's dangerous!" I added, still shaken by the encounter. We vowed to be more cautious, henceforth, avoiding future encounters with him, even if it meant coming home from school the roundabout way.

But we had not seen the last of Uyeki. Walking home from school one afternoon with Tancinco, a classmate of mine, he stopped in front of the derelict Roxy theater, fished a piece of chalk from one of his shirt pockets, and proceeded to draw on the wall a P-38 shooting down a Zero. Uyeki, who happened to be walking by on one his afternoon prowls, caught my friend red-handed.

"You come!" he barked at Tancinco, gripping him by the neck. Turning to me, he ordered: "You go home!"

As I reached the corner, I turned around to see Uyeki kicking Tancinco and beating him over the head, as they stumbled up Calle Real. Concerned, I decided to follow them from a distance. After much shoving and pushing, they eventually arrived at Kempitai Headquarters. I hid behind the bushes across the street from the building, to await developments.

Half an hour later, two soldiers emerged from the main gate, lugging a heavy sack between them. Grunting and swearing, they managed to suspend it from a low-lying limb of the huge acacia tree growing in their building's front yard. They then propped up a sign by the hanging sack and marched back into the building. I could barely make out the Japanese hieroglyphs from across the street but could not decipher them. From the occasional stirring in the sack, however, I suspected that Tancinco was in it.

The sign was like a magnet. Almost from the moment it was propped up, every soldier that happened by, would stop, and after reading it, would proceed to deliver a series of vicious kicks at the hanging sack before clubbing it with his rifle's butt. The sickening thuds started to make me ill. I grimaced at every blow until, gradually, the sign's message dawned on me. I knew I couldn't hide behind the bushes while my friend was being beaten senseless.

Suddenly, something in me bristled, tensed up, and finally snapped. Leaving the safety of my cover, I dashed across the street toward the hanging sack, picked up the sign and tore it up into shreds.

"You in there, Tan?" I asked, hoping that he wasn't. There was only a groan for an answer.

My move had not gone unnoticed. The sentry who was standing guard by the door started shouting at me. Wheeling around, I saw how, as if in slow motion, he cranked a bullet into his rifle's chamber, leveled it and took careful aim at me.

I froze.

There was no doubt in my mind that he was going to squeeze that trigger if I so much as breathed. Very slowly, I raised my arms in surrender.

The sound of voices inside the building was followed by a clatter of boots. Uyeki emerged a few seconds later, followed by two other Officers. All three of them had drawn their side arms. By then the sentry had overpowered me and flung me to the ground. One of his knees was digging painfully into the small of my back, as he yanked my head back violently by the hair.

"So! Young Spaniard want to pray hero!" Uyeki said sarcastically, as his sentry rudely raised me up to confront his Officer. I didn't realize, until I saw him there, face to face, just how much I loathed Uyeki.

"He didn't do anything!" I said, nodding toward the sack. "They're gonna kill him! You gotta take him down!" I blurted out incoherently.

"I don't gotta do nothing!" he sputtered, striking me repeatedly in the face with the back of his hand. "We shoot people for ress than he do!" he added irately. His face had turned beet red. I could tell he was working himself into a lather.

For a few tense moments, he just stood there, glaring at me in the waning afternoon light. Finally, he said: "You go home now! Next time you do something stupid rike this, we put you in sack, dipromat father or not!"

Obeying his nod, the guard released his grip on me and shoved me brusquely toward the street.

"Keep your head covered, Tan!" I whispered hoarsely in the direction of the sack, as I stumbled past it. This time there was no response.

That night at the dinner table, I had to make up a story about fisticuffs in school, to explain my two magnificent shiners. I knew Dad would have lodged an official complaint, had I told him the truth. That, I figured, would have only gotten both him and me in trouble. I was slowly learning the subtle and contradicting nuances of prudence and valor.

They must have hauled Tancinco down that evening because the sack was gone when I walked past the Kempitai Headquarters the next morning, on my way to school. He must have been pretty badly mauled because he never came back to school again.

5. GROWING UP PAINS

"Hermy?" asked Lawson, raising an eyebrow. He'd been reading the fight poster plastered on a wall bearing a 'Post No Signs' warning on it. "Kid Dingcong and Speedy Gomez are proper enough boxers' names, but Killer Hermy?"

"Yup," I answered evenly. "Sounded strange to me too until I found out his real name was Ermenegildo. Not a very snappy name for a boxer. Must'a changed it."

Suspecting I was pulling his leg, Lawson quietly dropped the subject, showing neither belief nor reservation. Deep down, though, I could tell he had his doubts. His intuition always stood him in good stead.

"These Filipinos really love their boxing, don't they?" he commented, changing the subject. "Not many heavyweights but, boy, those Flyweights and Bantamweights sure make up in quickness for their lack in heft."

Saturday afternoons, when there was a fight in town, we'd sneak under the tent flap of the makeshift boxing arena by the wharf and wormed our way to ringside. There, we'd lie low, ogling the glistening gladiators as they pranced about the squeaky boards, beating their brains out with cobra-like quickness and grace.

Boxing lessons thus learned, had to be practiced, and who better than with Iñaki Elordi. He was Basque, like I, but unlike my family's Pyrenean strain, his hailed from the Maritime Provinces. Though subtle, that was good enough reason to slug out our differences during recess, when the friars weren't watching. Iñaki was a bit of a runt, but he was a clever and feisty one. I can still taste the rusty smell of blood smearing my nose, these many years on. Our fisticuffs got to be so routine that the rest of the class soon wearied of watching them. Iñaki's older brother, Jon, would occasionally witness the fights, pretending to referee them. He'd slip me a punch, now and then, just to even things out.

Aggressiveness was not the only telltale sign of the onset of puberty, when I turned thirteen. Trembling on the brink of sex, the hormonal uproar awoke me to the confusing world of girls. There weren't that many of them around, so despite our Basque differences, Iñaki's sister, Karmele, became my belle. Something about the way she crinkled her eyes when she laughed stirred a strange kind of warmth in me. And there was an undeniable quiver every time we rubbed elbows or brushed hands when we walked together. I was badly smitten with Karmele.

Karmele was always surrounded by girl friends but occasionally, the two of us would coincide in Plaza Libertad, walking our dogs in the evening. Small talk did not come easily to Karmele. She was a little shy and had to be coaxed into conversation.

"How's things at the Sagrado Corazon?" I asked her, trying to break the conversational ice, the first time we stumbled upon each other at the Plaza. "The nuns still remember us?"

"I don't know about them, but I do!" she responded, blushing ever so faintly. "What I mean is the school's a lot quieter since you all left. No more of that turmoil you and Jesus Jimenez used to stir up. You two were perfectly awful!"

"Me?" I answered, feigning surprise. "I didn't do a thing! Jesus, maybe. He's still at it, you know, fomenting revolutions in San Agustin. But he's O.K. A little hyper perhaps, that's all."

Karmele laughed her haunting laugh. Sometimes, when walking close to each other, we'd hold hands. Watching her blush sent shudders of delight through me. Such innocence, I thought. I became increasingly and undeniably attracted to her, to the point of convincing myself that my feelings were so transparent that no words were needed to express them. I was sure she could sense them, the same way I thought I discerned a glimmer of reciprocity in her eyes.

But just when those evening walks promised to blossom into something more serious, the idyll was abruptly interrupted. Iñaki must have found out about our solitary evening walks because, quite unexpectedly, he started walking their dog in the evening, instead of Karmele. I was shattered.

"Boy, she's got pretty eyes!" I confessed to Jesus, one day. "Did'ja ever notice? They're grey-green. Kind'a like a cat's. I never saw anything like it."

My lovesick musings fell on deaf ears. "Yeah," remarked Jesus, "Her eyes are O.K., but did you check her legs!"

"You're crass!" I shot back, my Platonic affections offended by his remark. "You're always trying to sound so biggety, always parroting those brothers of yours. You don't even understand what they're saying half the time."

"And you're so naive!" he sniggered. "Just watch, you'll never get to first base with her. She's so shy it hurts. Besides, that Mari Kawayan she hangs around with is like her permanent shadow! Talk about albatrosses!"

I, too, had noticed Karmele's shyness, but, unlike Jesus, found it strangely appealing, that is, whenever I managed to be alone with her any more. She now seldom ventured out into the world unless escorted by a bevy of homely girlfriends. Maria Sarasola was her inseparable companion. Maria was friendly and outgoing enough, but so distressingly thin and gangly that Jesus nicknamed her 'Mari Kawayan,' or 'Bamboo Reed' Mary. Whoever doubled up with me on my lovelorn walks with Karmele was stuck with Mari Kawayan.

I turned to Lawson for help when Jesus Jimenez and Angel Arana, having had their fill of chaperoning, started insisting on swapping partners with me.

"It'll do your Spanish a world of good," I assured Lawson weakly. "I know she talks a blue streak but that's just what you need to improve your accent. Besides, you'd better start learning some civilized vocabulary. All those cuss words you're picking up from Jesus Jimenez have already gotten you into a heap of trouble at the dinner table."

"No thanks," he answered, leveling me with unblinking stare. "You keep her babble; I'll jolly well stick to my slang."

Our awkward approach to adolescent courtship was getting us nowhere fast. Unhappy at not having been invited to Mari Kawayan's birthday party, we sent her a frisky little white mouse inside a perforated shoebox, all neatly wrapped in gift paper. The shrieks we heard coming from her balcony in the middle of the party, confirmed our gift's intended effect. Iñaki Elordi told us later that the little critter had jumped onto the cakes and goodies when the girls opened the box, bringing their party to an abrupt end. Our names were mud with them, from then on.

There were dry, lovelorn weeks ahead, after the mouse episode. The girls played coy and hard to get, sniffing at us every time we approached them. I was so frustrated I even stopped picking on Iñaki for a while, hoping he'd ask me over to his house. That way, I schemed; I could get close to his sister and make up with her. He never caught on to the ruse, but didn't invite me, anyway.

Some weeks after the mouse fiasco, several Spanish girls blew into town from the nearby island of Cebu. "Relatives of the Burgas," reported Jesus Jimenez, all a-twit. "Here on a family visit, I understand. Haven't seen 'em yet but my brother Tony says they're knockout!"

They were good-looking alright and friendly to boot. There were four of them, ranging in age from thirteen to twenty. Word of their arrival had spread like wildfire and the atmosphere was suddenly thick with hormones. Every young Spanish male in town turned up, every afternoon after school, at the basketball court under the Burgas' living room window, posturing around the newcomers.

Our gang stumbled over each other, vying for Chiquita's favors. She was the youngest of the sisters and, we thought, the most fetching and vivacious of the lot. But we never got anywhere with her, despite our shamefaced courting displays. There were simply too many suitors and Chiquita played the infatuation field masterfully, pitting one's adolescent anguish against the others'.

Karmele and her friends, meanwhile, got their noses out of joint; it was we, now, who were ignoring them. However dubious, that was to be our only victory during the Vidarte interlude. The victory was short-lived, it turned out, because the Vidarte girls didn't stay long, returning home to the neighboring island of Cebu, shortly after. And so, we were, once again, left high and dry. Girls were out for a while, and we had to turn to other less frustrating distractions.

I didn't have long or far to search. Eusebio, one of the houseboys, owned a fighting cock which he kept tied up in a remote corner of the downstairs patio, over by the water well. He'd spend endless hours training it for battle. Restraining it by the tail with one hand, he'd slap its thighs with the other. The rooster soon developed a powerful set of thigh muscles, trying to escape the torment.

"Whyn't you take me with you to the cockfight some afternoon," I pleaded with him, sitting on my haunches next to him, observing the slapping ritual.

"Your mother not like it," he answered. "Not game for kids, anyhow." He was right about Mom's disapproval.

'Unedifying spectacle,' I could just hear her harrumphing. But my relentless pestering eventually broke down Eusebio's resistance. One Sunday afternoon, under cover of the siesta hour, he grudgingly took me along with him to the cockfight.

The indoor pen in the outskirts of town was crawling with men. The deafening roar died down a notch when we walked in. It suddenly dawned on me why Eusebio had been so reluctant to bring me along: I was probably the only European kid who'd ever set foot on that pit. The crowd eventually got used to my presence, however, and soon settled down to some serious shouting and betting.

Eusebio's cock was one of the first ones up in the fight roster. The small sharp knife he gingerly strapped onto one of the cock's talons looked like a small scythe, sharp and wicked-looking. At the referee's signal, the two men released their cocks from opposite ends of the circular sandpit.

Cawing apprehensively, the cocks approached each other warily. The distance between them gradually narrowed until, finally, they were confronting each other in the middle of the pit. Everyone held his breath; you could hear a pin drop. Suddenly, there was a blur of croaks and flying feathers, drowned, shortly after, by the howls of the approving crowd.

"*Sigue na!*" shouted Eusebio amidst the din, trying to encourage his fowl. But it was already too late. The small sharp knife strapped to the opponent's talon had slashed into Eusebio's gamecock's underbelly, spilling its entrails all over the sandpit. The doomed cock kicked convulsively up to its last life-twitch.

The excited crowd roared approval of the gory spectacle. After collecting their bets during the intermission, they splurged on *balút*, a favorite delicacy of half-fertilized chicken eggs. Eusebio bought one, cracked the top off and started munching on its contents.

"You wanna try?" he asked, offering me his half-sucked *balút* egg.

"No, thanks," I said, trying to repress the heaves at the sight of the wet, feathery mess he was offering me.

We didn't stay to watch the rest of the fights. Eusebio was glum. He didn't talk much on the way home, either. He'd spent a lot of time training that cock of his, and it was all for nothing. Now he looked about as crestfallen as the dead bird he was carrying under his arm, wrapped in a banana leaf. There would be chicken for dinner at the help's table that evening.

"Tough luck," I said, trying to commiserate with him. "Don't worry, you'll get another cock and have another go at it."

He shuffled along, unconvinced. "Rooster didn't crow this apternoon, when you come. Bad sign!" Like most country folk, Eusebio was superstitious. I could almost read his thoughts; my presence had hexed him.

As we came up on a huge Banyan tree growing over the sidewalk, Eusebio deliberately crossed to the other side of the street, giving the tree and its eerily-spreading branches a wide berth.

"Why'd you do that for?' I asked, puzzled by the maneuver.

"Bad luck to walk under Banyan tree." he said, looking back warily at the tree. "You get *pasmo* that way." I'd heard about '*pasmo*' before; it was a kind of paralysis that withered an arm or drooped half a face. "Sleeping without covers under the moonlight also give *pasmo*", he added.

And he had other weird, spooky legends, like the one about '*Paré waay ulu*,' the Filipino version of the Sleepy Hollow, except in this case the rider was a headless priest who galloped around in the night, chasing kids and hapless women.

Sudden, unexplained deaths were invariably blamed on someone's voodoo curse. The funerals that ensued were pathetic events, with wailing professional mourners shuffling behind the funeral carriage, beating their breasts, followed by a band playing mournful, Italian-sounding dirges. It was a sad affair; everyone cried.

Chinese funerals, on the other hand, were fun to watch, the mood almost festive. It was like a celebration. Orientals, dressed up in mourning white, would dance around the beribboned funeral float, tossing firecrackers at it and having a merry old time. If there were dancing girls waiting in the afterlife, the mood was properly set.

"What do you say we share the dead guy's meal tonight," I proposed to the gang, as we watched a Chinese funeral go by, one day. "Chinese leave food on the tomb to give nourishment to the spirit for its journey," I explained. "Kind'a like the Egyptians with their mummies."

"You don't wanna mess around with the dead," said Jesus, reluctantly. "Who knows, you might even stumble on *Pare waay Ulu* at the cemetery."

"Don't be a ninny!" said Lawson. "Bet those egg rolls taste great! Let's check 'em out."

The brazen plan was approved. We arranged to meet at the square's kiosk at midnight, when everyone was asleep. Jesus was apprehensive at first but finally agreed to join the Chinese pajama party.

"Why'd you bring Lobo for?" he asked when he arrived at the plaza, just as the church's clock tower struck midnight. "I don't see any point in bringing the German shepherd along," he groused.

"For protection," said Luis, trying not to smile. "They say dogs can spot ghosts a mile away. He'll warn us if there's one around." I could see Jesus' pupils dilating in the moonlight. The revelation had made him even warier than he already was, but he wasn't about to let on and managed to keep his peace.

A full moon lit our way through the deserted streets. Even the Japanese sentry that usually stood guard at the Capitol building's entrance had gone to bed. We walked briskly toward the outskirts of town, on the road to Jaro.

We got to the Chinese cemetery half an hour later. The half unhinged gates stood agape, in dubious welcome. I had half expected to smell the sweet scent of death inside, and was surprised, instead, by the faint smell of *Sampaguita* flowers wafting across the mausoleum-lined alleys. It struck me at first that there weren't any crosses anywhere in sight, until I realized that this wasn't the place for them; it was not, after all, a Christian cemetery.

"How're we gonna find this guy's tomb?" asked Jesus, speaking in hushes, as if trying not to awaken the dead around him. It was spooky enough, just letting sleeping Chinese lie.

"Follow your nose, simple," sniggered Lawson. I could tell he was starting to lose patience with Jesus' negative vibrations.

Lobo suddenly started barking. We all froze in place. I could feel the hairs on the back of my neck standing at pert attention. Jesus Jimenez' knees were audibly knocking against each other.

"Let's get the hell outta here!" he said, retreating toward the gate. Lobo's howls had leached away all pretenses at bravery.

"Wait," I said, as Lobo dashed off along one of the weed-choked alleys, barking frenziedly. "I think he's after some animal." That was just the way he and Iru used to take off after alley cats, years earlier.

Warily, we followed the dog, as he ran at full tilt, growling as he went. He disappeared behind a large mausoleum at the end of a row, but we could still clearly hear his barking. Turning the corner, we almost stepped on a pair of alley cats that whizzed past us in the moonlight, yowling in terror.

Lobo had just finished gobbling down the last tidbits of the Chinese farewell party, when we finally caught up with him. We tried to shoo him away from the plate but it was too late. He'd licked it clean.

"This bloke'll have to make the trip on an empty stomach," quipped Lawson, standing on the freshly dug mound.

"So will we," answered Jesus sourly. "Let's go."

Turning around, we walked home briskly, a little disappointed but happy to have tried, glowing with the small pride of fright endured and overcome.

But cockfights and cemetery outings were definitely not filling the Karmele void. I was seeing less and less of her, after Lawson had refused to run interference with Mari Kawayan. Our meetings were now reduced to chance encounters in church, during Sunday mass. The longing sideways glances cast across the aisle had become increasingly frustrating and unfulfilling.

My ears perked up when Jesus Jimenez and Angel Arana mentioned something about becoming altar boys. "You get to check the girls out at close quarters during Communion," Jesus assured us.

That sounded like a good enough reason to join the feeble ranks of acolytes at the San Jose Parish church. José Antonio Apellaniz, the Sacristan, taught us the altar ropes. It didn't take long to memorize the Latin responses but the beauty of the ancient liturgy totally escaped us. Occasionally, we'd trip up royally, like the time Jesus Jimenez slipped a response from the Mass of the Dead in the middle of what was supposed to be a joyous Baptismal ceremony.

"These times are out of joint, anyway. What do you expect?" he rationalized when the displeased Apellaniz berated him for the slip-up.

The Sisters of Charity must have forgotten our turbulent months with them a year earlier, or perhaps there just weren't enough acolytes around, because one day the good nuns asked Jesus Jimenez and me to serve Mass in their chapel, to celebrate the feast of the Immaculate Conception.

"How come they didn't ask Angel Arana?" I asked Jesus Jimenez.

"It's that sorry shadow of a moustache he's sporting lately," said Jesus. "Those nuns can smell lost innocence a mile away. They can't have any of that around those young wards of theirs. They're over-stimulated enough, as is!"

Fr. Pampols, their Chaplain, was his usual grumpy self, breathing mild oaths every time we blundered at the altar, like when we snuffed out his altar candles on cracking the side windows too wide, or ringing the altar chimes out of time.

"Watch this," whispered Jesus as he walked past me, before the Offertory. Standing at the foot of the altar, he faced the congregation and started swinging the smoking censer in their direction. He did it sedately enough at first, but soon got carried away, swinging it with increasing flair. I could tell he was showing off.

Fr. Pampols looked at him sideways and frowned. The next thing I knew, the censer's chain had snapped, launching the hot pot in a perfect ballistic trajectory over the girls' heads, spewing hot incense embers over the congregation. The censer smashed into one of the stained glass windows along the chapel's wall with clinking finality.

"Ee-e-e-k!" shrieked the girls, scrambling for cover, drowning out Sor Imelda's earnest chirping and the celebrant's Latin offerings.

"*Silencio, coño!*" roared Pampols with resounding authority, trying to quell the communal giggling.

The nuns never asked us back again after the apocalyptic disruption.

But there were other perks to altar boy-hood. Besides discretely dipping into the dwindling supply of consecration wine, there was the Communion liturgy to look forward to. Holding the paten under the communicant's jaw gave us a chance to gently tap our girlfriends' Adam's apple, as they received Communion.

"The paten's an absolute sine-qua-non if you thwack 'em hard enough with it," theorized Jesus Jimenez. The awkward maneuver did little to impress the girls.

Christmas time was the highlight of our altar boy year. The Parish priest sent Angel Arana, Jesus Jimenez and me out into the streets, dressed in our bright red robes and clean surplices, toting a crèche-sized figurine of the baby Jesus lying in a crib, for the townsfolk to kiss and pay homage to. We got to keep their monetary donations, which was the priest's way of compensating us for all the meager allowances of the preceding year of Sundays.

"*Pax Vobiscum!*" we proclaimed cheerfully on entering people's homes. The family lined up to kiss the baby's protruding leg, its color now faded from the wiped slobber of a thousand kisses. We stuffed the peso bills the housewives gave us in our pockets, thanked them with profuse *salamats*, and headed for the next home.

"O.K.," said Jesus, almost salivating. "Now for the grande finale!"

Our pace quickened visibly as we approached the town's red light district. Standing conveniently across the street from each other, were the town's two houses of ill repute, one Filipino, the other Korean. Like skittish Crusaders, we drew forbidden pleasure from walking into the whorehouses with religious sanction. Once inside, we gawked at the flimsily dressed prostitutes lolling about their living rooms, dressed in gaudy gowns and cheap trinkets.

Dim recollections of more modest days helped loosen the Filipino whores' purse strings. But being of an altogether different persuasion, the Korean prostitutes didn't even understand the mythology at hand. They looked on quizzically as we produced our peace offering. Not even our appeal to pity seemed to work. Despairing, Jesus Jimenez took a stab at their other more wordly interests.

"*Sukoshi ren ai ga hoshii desu,*" he spouted out falteringly, believing he was pleading for a little affection. The oriental women stared at him blankly. Confused by his mixed signals, the middle aged Madame finally showed us the door, without further ado.

"You're jejune!" I remarked as I walked past her on my way out. I had come across the funny sounding word in a novel I had just finished reading, its meaning totally escaping both the Madame and me. Only Jesus Jimenez chuckled appreciatively, suspecting I'd just come up with a new addition to our gibberish vocabulary.

As he walked out, the oriental harlot standing at the door made a playful pass at Jesus Jimenez' privates. Still savoring the lip-teasing 'jejune,' he failed to see the woman's sleight of hand, gave a start and almost dropped his crèche baby on the whorehouse floor. We laughed all the way to the Minami ice cream parlor, trying to visualize our limp explanations of the near catastrophe to the Parish priest.

"Not to worry," sniggered Jesus Jimenez. "We'll kill them with love next time," vowing to return the following year to convert the heathen.

6.   FIRST STIRRINGS

More than two years had passed since the Iru and Tancinco incidents, and yet their memories, silently kneaded, kept gurgling up, naggingly reminding me of unfulfilled promises. Though long nurtured, both the timing and the execution of their redress came quite unexpectedly.

The British-owned Hongkong & Shanghai National Bank turned out to be the unlikely grounds for my first open act of defiance against the Japanese Army. Shortly after the invasion, the Japanese had sealed all foreign banks and frozen their assets. Prominently pasted on their padlocked doors, were posters threatening stiff punishment to trespassers. But I'd been around Jesus Jimenez long enough to know that little thou-shalt-nots only made forbidden enterprises that much more enticing.

Living next door to the British bank, Jesus was, inevitably, recruited to help size up the job. The prospects of havoc made him salivate.

"This is going to be a cake-walk," he admitted confidently. "Just leave it to me. I know all about Banks. Dad's the president of one, remember?"

Although his arguments did little to still our doubts, Lawson, Luis, the Arana brothers and I reluctantly followed him into the forbidden bank one afternoon. Scaling the moldy, glass-spiked garden walls, we gained access to the grounds, breaking into the abandoned building through a hesitant back door.

"Dad used to be friends with this Bank's president," reminisced Lawson, once we had gained entry into the dining room. "This guy was some kind of weird bachelor. Used to dress up every evening in black tie. Ate all by himself on this table right here, with lit candelabra, and servants, all gloved up and liveried. The works," he said, passing his hand over the enormous Molabe hardwood table, hewn out of a single massive log.

After dancing a jig on it, we bounced up and down on the leather sofas and finally laid ourselves down on the huge canopied bed in one of the guest bedrooms. Jesus Jimenez pretended he was snoring. He even broke wind, which he could do at will, just to be funny.

"Gross!" muttered Lawson, disgustedly. Pedro Mari Arana's giggles only prompted a second toot from Jesus Jimenez. The young Arana brother had yet to learn that Jesus had to be ignored, when he was cutting up like that. So Lawson ribbed him, unsubtly.

Rummaging through the well-appointed quarters in the mansion's second floor, Luis suddenly came upon a secret panel in one of the master bedroom's closets.

"Hey guys, take a look!" he said, hailing us over to the door. Pushing it open, the door swung with a sinister squeak into a dark and narrow passage.

"This is right spooky," whispered Lawson with mounting concern. He was starting to have second thoughts about the adventure, more worried now about the prospects of being caught than for having intruded on hollowed British ground.

"Don't be a ninny," said Jesus with feigned serenity. "We've got one of these secret passageways in our bank ourselves. They're great for fast getaways."

The need for hurrying in and out of bank bedrooms puzzled Lawson. "You've watched one matinee serial too many," he remarked mockingly. He never trusted Jesus Jimenez farther than he could throw him.

Striking a match, we followed the dim passageway until we reached a spiral staircase that wound dizzily down to what looked like the bank's main vault. Fashioning a torch out of some papers that were lying on the floor, we investigated the vault's clammy interior by torchlight. Judging from its warped surface and distorted hinges, the Japanese had been trying, unsuccessfully, to blow the huge steel door open, with explosive charges.

We could have saved them the trouble; all we found inside the cavernous vault were packets of cancelled checks, all neatly stacked along its walls. Picking one up, I tried reading the checks by torchlight.

"Hey, this is Dad's handwriting!" I exclaimed, recognizing his small, neatly strung-out calligraphy. The cancelled checks, most of which bore his signature, were bound in fist-sized packets, flimsily held together by a thin, single-twist wire. It didn't take much imagination to recognize their potential for play ammunition, a suspicion quickly confirmed on watching one of the hurled packets explode on contact with the wall, dramatically sun bursting checks all over the place.

We lugged armfuls of them up the spiral stairway, stockpiling them in different strategic locations around the house. The battle was soon joined, without bothering with the niceties of alliances or coalitions. Blurred by flurries of strewn paper, the epic free-for-all waxed and waned all afternoon, with classic indecision. Someone gained control of the high ground temporarily, only to be dislodged from it moments later, by someone else. The noisy skirmishes raged up and down every floor, in and out of every room of that forbidden battleground. It was a glorious, long-to-be-remembered melee.

When we finally left the premises that evening, every single room of the building, especially the marble floor of the bank's rotunda, was littered with the debris of battle. We could only guess the surprise on the inscrutable Japanese faces when they realized, on seeing all those calling cards, that someone had beaten them to the punch at the vault, and had had a roaring good time, while at it.

We visited the bank several times after that first raid, but it wasn't the same any more. When we finally ran out of packets of cancelled checks, we decided to inspect the main offices on the ground floor. Figuring it was our patriotic duty to relieve the Japanese of their ill-got gains, we picked up all the bank stationary and office supplies we could stuff into our shirts and pant pockets. We were even considering requisitioning one of the office typewriters when we suddenly heard a car parking outside the Bank's main gate.

"We better bug outta here," said Jesus, when someone started rattling the padlocked chain on the main gate, moments later. Scrambling over the office's sliding accordion doors, we sprinted for the open garden and made a fast vaulting exit over the fence, to safety.

A sentry was permanently posted at the Bank's front door after that last raid, discouraging any further foray into the British bank.

"That's one less soldier at the front," commented Lawson Davies sourly.

We didn't have long to wait for our next attempt at sabotage. As with the first, the opportunity came unbidden. I was watching several *parao* sailboats land on the beach one afternoon, near where we had just fought one of our bruising sand ball battles. Having just read a Tom Swift seafaring adventure novel, my mind was wandering with nautical thoughts when one of them suddenly bubbled up into consciousness.

"Hey, let's build a sailboat like that one there," I proposed to Lawson, pointing at one of the *paraos*. "Just you and me."

His eyes lit up instantly. Here was a chance to build something fun and practical, a thought to make a budding engineer grin. In good Scottish tradition, Lawson was slowly developing into a mechanical wizard. Gifted at fixing things, he simply could not resist prying gadgets open and taking appliances apart, just to probe their innards and see what made them tick. Amazingly, he could reassemble them without leftover parts, most of the time, anyway.

"We could even sail to Guimarás with it!" he suggested, turning the idea around in his head and savoring it with obvious relish.

This was the small island we could see from the beach, across the sun-bright strait, no more than three miles distant. *Paraos* with colorful sails sailed from our beach to the green island every day, plying the waters with grace and easy speed. Sometimes, we'd cling to their outriggers for as long as we dared, until it was almost too far to swim back to shore.

"The name sounds Portuguese," puzzled Lawson. "I didn't think their discoverers ever got this far."

"I don't think they did, either. The mapmaker who named that island must have been a relative of that other Italian who managed to get America named after himself without even having ventured out to it."

"Pretty sneaky lot, those Italians!" commented Lawson. "Columbus was Italian too."

"Yes, well," I said trying to change the subject. "Let's just get started on this boat right away before some Italian gets a jump on us," I suggested, now caught up in the excitement of the enterprise.

"There's still plenty of corrugated tin roofing lying around in the burned part of town. That should do for hull material. We've also got plenty of wood for the ribbing and bamboo for the outriggers." In my mind's eye, I already saw a small and graceful *parao*, capable of carrying at least two passengers.

Rummaging through the rubble near the burnt-out warehouses by the wharf, we selected the least damaged piece of tin roofing we could find, and dragged it home. Hammering its corrugations flat, we shaped it into a hull, riveting the bow end together and nailing the stern end to a semicircular piece of wood.

For seating and structural support, we nailed several wooden slats to the midsection of the hull. We then attached bamboo poles to each end of two wooden outriggers. The shipbuilding thus concluded, we painted the hull with generous coats of pitch to plug up its many nail holes and ensure seaworthiness. Two weeks after the keel-laying ceremony, she was finally ready for her maiden voyage.

"Funny how seamen refer to ships as 'shes' and 'hers'," I observed, gazing admiringly at our handiwork. "It's kinda tender and respectful, don't you think?"

"Sounds more like mistrust to me," commented Lawson. "It's like the sea; they talk about its bosom like something one sinks into. Sailors are such a horny lot!"

It was getting dark at noon. A storm with all the makings of a typhoon was starting to rage outside, driving the first brittle rain against our eyes. Being her Ship-owner and self-appointed Captain, I decide, against my First Mate's better judgment, to conduct the launching ceremonies on the very next day.

"Bet this is going to be another Armada all over again," warned Lawson, alluding to the elements Phillip of Spain had blamed for the sinking of his Armada, several centuries earlier. "You Spaniards never learn, do you?" he added wryly.

"Oh yeah!" I huffed. "Spaniards were a lot better sailors than the Brits," I added testily. "We were first to sail around the world, remember? By a good half century, as I recall!"

"Aye aye, Cap'n," said the Scot, disengaging. The hint of sarcasm in his voice irritated me almost as much as the 'Rule Britannia' he had started whistling.

The rain and bluster did not stop the ship's christening ceremony, the next morning. Lacking a proper champagne bottle, we simply relieved ourselves onto its glistening black hull, ceremoniously peeing at it, even against the now howling wind.

"I christen thee Sea Hawk," I said solemnly, remembering an Errol Flynn movie, where the dashing swashbuckler with the prissy little moustache singlehandedly tore up fleets of galleons, all up and down the Spanish Main.

Despite Lawson's growing misgivings, we dragged the boat along the sand to the edge of the angry sea. Waiting for a monster wave to crash, we manhandled her into the wind-tossed waters, quickly clambered aboard and started paddling furiously out to sea.

The water curled around the boat with threatening voices. Topping the first of several mountainous waves, we howled wildly back at the wind as the tiny boat teetered on the wave's top and then disappeared into its back trough. The waterlogged boat quivered almost to the top of the next wave but didn't quite make it this time. The huge wave swamped us, snapping one of the outriggers in half.

"Row! Row harder, yeoman!" I shouted above the storm.

The water was now up to our necks. Half bemused by our predicament, we rowed in useless circles, laughing between lungfuls of saltwater until a gigantic wave finally flipped the wounded boat over, slamming it against the beach with wet finality. We lay there laughing, our boat a sorry shambles. We finally dragged its remains up to high ground, a bit disappointed but otherwise unbowed. Lawson was kind enough to refrain from reminding me he'd told me so.

We repaired the broken outrigger, tightened a few nuts and bolts and tried again, after the storm had abated, several days later. The voyage may not have been her maiden attempt any longer but we declared the trials a smashing success, anyway, proclaiming the boat seaworthy. We sailed her tentatively around the breakwaters, rowing back and forth to get the hang of it.

Lawson and I spent many happy hours on the Sea Hawk. Guimarás was still in the future, the island a bit too distant to try yet. We'd have to design a sail, first, and then learn to navigate with it. Even without a rig, the vessel handled a bit awkwardly. There had to be many intermediate trials before attempting Guimarás.

"Let's make a commando raid!" I suggested during one of our outings, shortly after our maiden voyage. Lawson stopped rowing, his ears perking up visibly.

"Where?" he asked, now on pins and needles.

"You know that little beach about half a mile east of here, near Fort San Pedro? The one just east of the breakwaters that's supposed to be off limits? I saw the Japs unloading boxes there from trucks the other day, when we were playing in the deserted private airfield just north of there. I think it must be an ammunition dump or something."

"Smashing!" he exclaimed, warming up to the thought. It didn't take much to get Lawson up on an excited state, especially when there was anything afoot even faintly promising adventure.

We fashioned a sail from a sheet we borrowed from the linen closet, sewing its ends to a pair of shorn broomsticks. We then rigged it up onto a long wooden mast which we had smartly stuck through a hole drilled through the boat's center slat, and battened down with guy wires. Having provisioned and made the boat ready on the eve of the journey, we pushed off at dawn, one Saturday morning, on our way to the forbidden beach.

There wasn't much of a breeze in the early morning so we paddled around aimlessly for a while. Soon, a mild flurry kicked up, filling the sail out and tugging us gently on our way. The light breeze on my face made me realize that we had created motion by coaxing nature to do our work for us. The thought filled me with a sense of small pride and wonder.

Poking about among the coves, I felt like a pirate in search of hidden treasure, looking for a spot to land. Half an hour later, we slipped into the chosen inlet and glided quietly into the off-limits beach. Taking the sail down after scraping bottom, we crouched behind the dunes for a few moments, speaking in whispers, listening for telltale sounds. We could only hear the rhythmic slap of wavelets behind us, their white froth leaving their lacework on the solitary black sand. Far above us, a seagull cried out with all the urgency of a yawn.

Reassured by the surrounding quiet, we craned our necks to peek through the cattail reeds growing on the shimmering dunes. There, less than a hundred yards away, a Japanese sentry sat stolidly on a stack of tarpaulin-covered boxes, facing out to sea, in our general direction. He had not seen us. With a rifle resting easy on his lap, he yawned occasionally, picking at his nose with bored insistence.

"These Japs sure take this war business seriously, don't they," I whispered to Lawson.

"Yeah! The sod is sure mucking up our commando operation fast," muttered Lawson, disgusted by the prospects of our raid rapidly turning into a harmless picnic.

"Don't fret. There'll be other times for glory," I predicted, munching on one of the bananas we'd brought along for lunch. "Next time we go there," I whispered, pointing at the dark green mountains of Guimarás to the East. "We've got to study these currents before we do that, though. We sure wouldn't wanna be swept off to Borneo, or somewhere!"

"We'll make it," rejoined Lawson, perking up. "If the *paraos* do it, the Sea Hawk will too, by George!" he exclaimed, carried away by the nautical thought. I raised a finger to my lips motioning silence, worried that his excitement would compromise our cover.

It was a needless gesture; the sentry was now fast asleep. He remained sitting up, arms on the rifle resting on his knees, dead to the world of strife. The tropics weren't a half bad place for military duty, he must have been musing.

We slipped out of the cove as quietly as we had sailed into it, but this time we only used our paddles, keeping a low profile, lest the sentry spot the sail and start shooting at us. We had noticed, lately, that the occupation troops were getting increasingly edgy. Probably, things weren't quite going their way any longer. The thought pleased us immensely.

7. SABOTAGE

"What's this?" asked Lawson, as we dragged the Sea Hawk over the top of the dunes, for an early morning sail. A strange, abandoned boat wallowed in the water, near where we usually shoved off. The filmy layer of oil lapping around it had left a dark slick on the sand.

"Looks like a lifeboat!" he said excitedly.

"'Haru Maru'," I read out loud, when I got close enough to decipher the Hiragana hieroglyphs on the lifeboat's identification plaque. "Sounds like a Jap Merchant Marine ship. Torpedoed by the Yanks, no doubt!"

"Look! Some of the survivors must'a got hurt!" said Lawson, pointing at the bloodstained bandages floating in the bilge water at the bottom of the lifeboat. "Their ship did get hit! Probably sunk, too!"

Dad's clandestine radio had been keeping us abreast of MacArthur's hop-scotching across the Pacific islands, during the preceding two years. The Philippines now lay athwart the American spearhead aimed at Japan. The lifeboat was our first real evidence that the Americans were approaching. The tide had definitely turned against the Japanese.

"Dad says American subs have been landing arms and stuff for the guerrillas in the islands for quite some time now," I remarked. "This here sinking proves they're close by; the thought filled me with indefinable joy.

"Yeah," said Lawson. "Mr. Jimenez says they're flooding the market with so much counterfeit, our 'funny money' is gonna be worthless before long."

"Good! That should knock the stool out from under this puppet government! Wonder how much longer they're gonna feed us this pap about 'Southeast Asia Co-Prosperity Sphere' and 'Asia for the Asiatics' bunk."

"Those guerillas are sure getting frisky, aren't they?" commented Lawson. "Dad thinks they're eventually gonna push the Japs out of their inland enclaves and force them to fall back on Iloilo."

"Yeah, that's probably why we're seeing more troop activity around town these days," I remarked. "You realize what that means, don't you? We'll be stuck here with them, with nowhere to go. Now we're really trapped!"

"So, what's new? It's been that way all along, hasn't it?" commented Lawson, philosophically. "No telephones, no mail, no passage in or outta here, no nothin'. Probably there'll just be a little less elbow room from here on out, that's all."

"Food is what worries me, though," I commented. "It's scarce enough now but it's bound to get worse if those guerrillas start tightening the noose."

The comment was like a self-fulfilling prophecy. A band of trigger-happy Filipino irregulars, armed to the teeth with new American arms, had started to close in on the city, just itching to come in for the kill. By the summer of 1944, we were literally besieged, hostages to a horde of cornered Japanese troops who had swollen the population of a beleaguered city, already overflowing with humanity.

The sudden influx of troops into town made the already severe housing problem critical. Early, one September afternoon, the Japanese Commander stopped by for an unfriendly visit.

"You must vacate the premises," he said in almost flawless English, in a voice as deep as Dad's. "We've chosen your residence for our headquarters," he continued, in a tone that brooked little dissent. "You have one week to vacate the premises." Raising a hand to his Colonel's field cap in a half-hearted salute, he turned around and was gone. Dad hadn't even had a chance to put a word in edgewise, it all happened so quickly.

"What do we do now?" asked Mom, with a note of despair. "I'm afraid we won't be able to find a place to stay." I'd never seen her so worried before. What she said next revealed the depth of her concern. "Being without a home scares me. There's something naked and obscene about roofless-ness," she added. "Surely, you'll find a way out of this scrape. You always do."

They had married at a fabled time in history when even women knew that men knew best.

Dad remained silent throughout her emotional monologue. "Don't worry," he answered in a calm, soothing voice, trying to reassure her. "I'll look around for vacancies in town, but I'm afraid the Japanese may have taken them all by now." After a brief pause, he added: "Probably one of the schools will let us use their facilities temporarily."

It did not sound promising.

The following days saw a flurry of activity around the house. Suitcases were packed and essentials crated for the move. The flight to the hills of Igbarás, three years earlier, had taught us the importance of light baggage and loose clothing. But having to choose between heirlooms to keep and mementos to discard was no less wrenching now than it had been the first time around.

Mom was quite fond of her chinoiseries, and clung to them through thick and thin. The large rosewood chest, inlaid with soapstone figurines of fierce-looking Chinese warlords, was once more packed to bursting with medicines and canned foodstuffs. The Chinese rugs were also readied for the pilgrimage. Luis and I had played on them, as children, driving our toy cars over their alien landscapes, crisscrossed by bridges and intricate road designs. They were like security blankets for us now.

As the week went by, it became increasingly apparent that Dad's attempts at finding lodgings would be fruitless. When the day of reckoning finally arrived, we still had no idea where we were moving to. We just sat around the loaded carts, mute as ponies in the rain, waiting for the Colonel to turn up and evict us. A sense of resigned hopelessness hung over the group.

As we sat there waiting, I became gradually aware of a distant droning. It sounded like a flight of bumble bees, at first, growing louder and louder until, finally, the hum of reciprocating engines became distinctly audible. The last time I'd heard anything like it had been three years earlier, when a flight of Japanese airplanes had approached Iloilo, on their first bombing run.

A rumbling noise, very much like that of distant thunder, reached us a few moments later. Eyes wide with apprehension, Luis and I eyed each other. Above us, the big chandelier started wobbling to and fro, its glass nodules jiggling randomly, filling the room with their eerie tinkling sounds. A fine dust had started settling gently all around us.

"Bombs!" cried Dad in a hoarse voice. "Downstairs, everybody!" he ordered, leading the way to the makeshift shelter under the main stairwell. As people bounded down the stairs, stumbling over each other, I made one quick detour to the living room windows, where a bizarre scene greeted my eyes. American warplanes were swooping down on a platoon of soldiers caught marching out in the open. The troops scattered, helter-skelter, ducking in and out of portals, ignoring their Officers' barked commands. The scene boggled the mind wonderfully. I was so engrossed in it all that Dad's voice, booming up at me from the stairwell, almost failed to register.

"Corsairs and Hellcats!" I told the huddled crowd, when I finally joined them in the shelter. "Scared the pants off of the

Japs! You should'a seen them running! Looked like a bunch of scared chickens! It was beautiful!"

"You could have gotten killed!" reproved Dad. "Don't ever tarry like that again."

Ambulance sirens rent the acrid afternoon air with their mournful wails, shortly after the planes left. There had been no air raid warning; the Leyte landing was still a month off, and no one had expected a raid that soon.

That was to be the first of an endless string of bombings to follow. Odd to say, the raids became a cause for quiet celebration, despite the teeth-jarring explosions and the occasional twinge of terror. The Americans were nearby, and the long-awaited liberation was just around the corner now. Or so we thought.

Pressed now by other more serious concerns, the Colonel called off his eviction orders. We all gave a collective sigh of relief when his Adjutant dropped by to relay the message, a day later. Mom relaxed a bit. She even eased up on her rosaries, but not much.

But the development that made our young hearts leap the most was the unexpected suspension of classes. The forced vacation offered vast possibilities. With the Japanese distracted by the bombings and the ever-tightening guerrilla noose, time seemed ripe for devilment, perhaps even a little sabotage. Fr. Budul's worn aphorism about the devil finding work for idle hands could now be put to the test. Besides, there were promises to keep with Iru and Tancinco. Like wood worn by many hands, revenge had lain in my mind, quiescent but carefully kneaded.

Air raids occurred like clockwork now, almost as predictably as horses turning their backs to the wind. A flight of carrier planes would turn up at mid morning, almost every day, pound military objectives around town and then leave, half an hour later. Almost invariably, the fighter-bombers dropped their last bomb load on the ships moored along the waterfront.

Living only a stone's throw away from the Iloilo River, we'd walk over to the wharf after the bombings, to appraise the damage. Occasionally, we'd see a smoldering steamer lying on its side, looking like some confused whale, puzzling over the fire in its belly. Before the sentries could shoo us away, we'd notice that the small launches docked along the waterfront always seemed to survive the pounding, unscathed.

"Too small," reasoned Lawson. "Probably not worth a bomb. The Yanks probably think they're just fishing boats. Don't even realize they're armed and harass the guerrillas on their patrols."

"Well, let's check 'em out," I proposed. "Those sentries wouldn't be hanging around unless there's something of value to be guarded. They'd be at the front, otherwise."

"Jolly good!" exclaimed Lawson. "Let's ask the rest of the gang," he proposed. "The more, the merrier."

I didn't think a mob scene at the waterfront was such a hot idea, especially when stealth was of the essence. But I relented after the list of invitees had been whittled down to just Jesus Jimenez and the Arana brothers.

"We can skip out of the house unnoticed after supper," suggested Luis, sounding very much like a seasoned conspirator. "It's full moon tonight," he added.

Dusk found us crouching behind a pile of rotting logs in a dark alley leading to the waterfront. A full moon splashed its wet silver on the murky river. Two sentries were marching up and down the waterfront, in opposite directions. Their long rifles seemed even longer and more ominous, with their affixed bayonets shining dully in the moonlight. We watched them make several rounds so we could figure out how long it took them to come full circle, meet again, smartly about-face, and start all over again.

The tension mounted as we waited. It was hard to keep our voices down, huddling there in the shadows, teetering on the edge of danger, waiting for the moment of final commitment. Just as the clock in the San Jose Church tower struck midnight, Lawson stood up to relieve himself, inadvertently sprinkling Pedro Mari Arana on the leg.

"Oh crap!" howled Pedro Mari disgustedly, before someone muzzled him.

Meanwhile, Jesus Jimenez, who was crouching nearby, reached over in the dark and, like a judge meting swift punishment, flicked Lawson's offending member.

"Gorblime!" muttered Lawson in pain, cupping his privates in his hands, furious at the unexpected judgment. "I'll get you for this, you little desiccated goober!" he snarled at Jesus Jimenez, scrambling toward him.

"Hey, you guys, knock it off!" I whispered hoarsely, interposing myself between the two of them. "You're gonna get us all in trouble any minute now!"

"You bloody dork!" persisted Lawson, still holding on to his benumbed privates, glowering at Jesus Jimenez.

It took a while but they eventually simmered down. Fortunately, the Japanese sentries had been out of earshot during the altercation. The next time the soldiers met again and started marching in opposite directions, I knew it was time to make our move.

"Let's go!" I whispered, leading the crouching group out into the open. For a moment, I wished that the moonlight hadn't been so bright.

Reaching the waterfront, we slithered toward the nearest launch. Jumping smartly onto its deck, which was flush with the wharf, we laid low behind the gunwale for a few seconds, making sure no one was on board, before crawling into the wheelhouse. Flushed with the thrill of deadly enterprise, we started rummaging feverishly through the boxes and drawers.

"Wow! Take a look at this!" whispered Luis in muffled excitement.

He had just pried open the lid of a heavy wooden box lying by the helm. There, before us, lay a long belt of neatly stacked machine gun bullets shining dully in the moonlight, fairly begging to be taken. Stuffing our pockets full with them, we jumped stealthily back onto the wharf and crouched, Indian file, toward the next boat, emptying our pockets into the river, bullet by bullet, as we went.

We had relieved several boats of their ammunition in this fashion, before Lawson first sounded the alarm.

"Hey guys," he warned hoarsely. "Think I hear 'em coming! We'd better piss off kind'a sharpish!"

Jumping out of the boat, we dashed for the shadows just as the sentries loomed out of the mists, their muffled footsteps now increasingly audible. Without a backward glance, we made a beeline for home.

It was hard going to sleep that night, for all the adrenalin overflow. We had discovered a way to hit back at the enemy, where it made a difference. Sitting up in bed, we went over the night's events, savoring and magnifying every detail, sensing that we had undergone some rite of initiation, crossed that dark-bright threshold into adulthood.

"It wasn't that difficult was it," said Luis. He was only twelve but already an accomplished saboteur.

"Piece'a cake!" crowed Lawson. "We've gotta do something more 'grown up' next time, though." We all agreed that our war effort needed embellishment.

"Sabotage must be like scratching," I commented, drowsily, just before dozing off. "It's hard to stop, once you get started."

The next opportunity for sabotage was not long coming. It happened on the small abandoned airfield at the eastern tip of town, not far from our earlier failed amphibious assault on the depot near Fort San Pedro. We'd been playing Cowboys and Indians all afternoon and were about to call it a day when we suddenly heard the rumble of vehicles. It was an odd time of day for military activity in that end of town, we thought, as we crouched and waited.

Soon after, we saw several trucks driving up and parking at the opposite end of the potholed runway, where we'd been playing. Craning our necks above the tall, dry Cogon grass, we observed several soldiers unloading gasoline drums from the parked vehicles. They subsequently covered the drums with dry grass, presumably to hide them from air reconnaissance. We watched the operation keenly, speaking in hushes.

"That must be the last of their remaining fuel for that rattletrap Zero they still have," I commented.

Thanks to an effective camouflage job, a lonely Zero fighter had managed to survive the Americans' daily aerial pounding of the military airport in Jaro, north of town. The solitary Japanese fighter would patrol the harmless skies in the evenings, when it was safe to fly unchallenged. Only a week earlier, however, a straggler P-38 had jumped it on its leisurely evening patrol. Attracted by the odd maneuvers directly above me, I had climbed the narrow iron ladder leading from the upstairs patio to the roof, to observe the dogfight from a better vantage point.

Like a pesky terrier nipping at the heels of a bigger, more cumbersome opponent, the Zero was flying spirals around the Lightning. It reminded me a little of Iru and the Colonel's horse in the park, years earlier. Whenever the Lightning got into trouble, it simply nosed upward in an almost vertical power climb, screaming off into the higher sky, easily out-flying the more nimble but slower Zero.

After a few uneventful exchanges of bursts, the two planes had peeled off in opposite directions, apparently running short of either fuel or ammunition. Crestfallen, I had watched my very favorite warplane climbing empty handed into the lofty afternoon. The Zero had limped toward the western sky, coughing and wheezing, but unscathed.

"Let's set the drums on fire," Lawson suggested, surprised at his own temerity.

"How do you expect to do that without getting shot at, you dipstick!" asked Jesus, not too keen on the brazen plan.

"Don't get shirty!" retorted the Scot, unhappy with the exposed loose ends of his proposed strategy.

"Probably we can just set this end of the field on fire," I interposed. "The Cogon grass is bone dry and it's bound to go up like wildfire. The wind's blowing in the right direction. Sooner or later it'll get to the drums."

The juvenile Council of War reached a quick consensus. Jesus Jimenez, who was always snitching Akebono cigarettes from his dad, provided the matches. After the trucks had left, he set a match to the dry grass on our end of the airfield. Not waiting to admire our handiwork, we hot-footed it for home.

Half an hour later, a series of muffled explosions interrupted supper. Feigning surprise, all three of us stood up from the table and rushed over to the living room windows. Clouds of black smoke billowed upward in the blood-red sky above the deserted airfield.

Moments later, a solitary Japanese fire truck rushed to the scene, siren wailing balefully. It was too late. The last of the Japanese aviation fuel in the island of Panay had literally gone up in smoke.

We never saw the Zero fly again.

8.   DANGEROUS GAMES

Shortly after the Leyte landing, American warplanes started bombing military objectives around town in daily earnest, adding considerably to the dull excitement of the besieging guerrillas' deadly sideshow. Dad ordered a proper shelter built in one of the corners of the house's ground floor, thus adding to the protection already provided by the building's massive walls. For added safety, layers of sandbags were piled up on top of the squat, heavy-timbered structure.

We got so used to the sound of approaching airplanes that we could hear them coming long before the sirens sounded the alarm. The raids had become so routine that they bred in me an unhealthy contempt for safety. I soon started ignoring the sirens altogether, dawdling upstairs to watch the fireworks, each time from a different vantage point around the house. The best observation spot, I soon discovered, was the kitchen stairway's open landing, with its unobstructed view of the wharf, only a few hundred yards away. That was where the action usually took place.

Loitering there one day, I observed a half dozen F4U-4 Corsairs gaining altitude in the distant sky before gracefully peeling off, one by one, on their final southerly approach. The planes were drawing a bead on a ship docked in the wharf, almost directly in front of me. As I watched the little spits of flame spewing out of each wing's leading edge, something in the back of my mind warned me that I was courting danger, perhaps even taunting death. I remember just standing there, glued to the landing, washed by a strange feeling of terror mixed with the insane joy of daring.

"Bird watching has nothing over warplane watching," I confessed to Lawson and Luis, later that afternoon, "especially when you're on the receiving end of a fire-spouting Vought Corsair."

"That's why Generals live to be old farts," Lawson commented wryly. "They don't hang around the front lines too long; makes for a ripe old age."

But even air raids grew humdrum, after a while. After the noonday bombings, we gradually started venturing farther and farther afield from the shelter. Fooling around on one of those unsanctioned outings, Luis and Angel Arana were rolling an empty oil drum down Plaza Libertad one afternoon, creating a rumbling noise that sounded just like approaching aircraft. A Japanese Sergeant, who happened to be drilling his troops in the town square, heard the noise and started bellowing orders to his troops:

"Hikoki arimasu!"

Thus warned of approaching aircraft, the soldiers lost no time jumping into the foxholes that pockmarked the square. Oblivious of the commotion they were stirring, meanwhile,

Luis and Angel Arana continued rolling their drum down the street,

Realizing their false alarm, the soldiers climbed out of their foxholes and lit out after Luis and Angel to settle face-loss accounts. When they finally caught up with them, they became so engrossed in kicking and knuckle-rapping the two boys that they failed to notice four P-39 Air cobras that were swooping down on them at that very moment, from out of the clear blue sky.

When the bullets started raking the ground around them, the soldiers disengaged and dove right back into their foxholes. Serpentining their way across the park, Luis and Angel ducked into the baptistery of the nearby San Jose church, while the planes continued to strafe the soldiers outside. Several stray bullets gouged large chunks of plaster from the front of the church. One of them whizzed through the baptistery window, where Luis and Angel had ducked into, singing Luis on the neck just before smashing into the baptismal font and splintering it into a thousand marble shards.

Padre Jesus, the parish priest, jumped out of his confessional, face rough with rage. When Luis explained that they were being strafed by Bell Air cobras, something inside the priest snapped. Struggling with profanity, he dashed out of the church, raised a fist at the departing airplanes, and vented his outrage.

"Aero-*Cabras!*" he shrieked in damaged agitation, as if 'air-goats!' were the ultimate exorcism he could fling at the winged heathen.

Luis' close call rattled the household when details leaked out at the dinner table, that evening. Though a band-aid sufficed to dress his neck bruise, the incident drastically clipped our mobility henceforth.

The grounding forced us to device new ways of harassing the enemy; now it had to be from close quarters. Only a few days after the drum incident, Lawson and I lobbed a 500-Watt light bulb at two sentries patrolling the street below us. Startled by the explosion, they whipped around to confront their assailants. Finding the street deserted, they looked up at our windows, suspiciously. Lawson and I froze behind the slats. After what seemed an eternity, the despondent soldiers finally resumed their patrol, much to our relief.

During the long grounding interlude, those living room windows were to become our primary observation post. From dawn till dusk, we'd watch Japanese soldiers as they went about their daily routine, starting with early morning calisthenics to evening ablutions. Stripped down to their loincloths, they'd devote half an hour every morning, at dawn, to strenuous in-place exercises, repeating shouted commands with great abandon. Evenings, they'd line up for supper, which consisted of a bowlful of rice, graced by a single solitary sardine. The frugal menu never varied.

Bayonet practice was always a hair-raising spectacle. "These guys must be awesome at hand-to-hand combat," I commented one afternoon, watching them thrust their long bayonets into the bellies of straw dummies propped up in the middle of the street, shouting 'Banzai!' as they lunged forward.

"Yeah, those bayonets are spooky enough, even without all the shrieking. They'd scare hell outta me!" remarked Lawson.

"They sure shout a lot, don't they," commented Luis. "Probably a little hard of hearing, from all the shouting."

"They're all born a little deaf!" Jesus Jimenez volunteered, one afternoon he came visiting. "The same taut facial muscles that make 'em squinty-eyed also squinch up their eardrums. It's tough hearing with drawn eardrums. That's why they have to shout so."

"Bugger off!" muttered Lawson, unable to repress a smile at the nonsense Jesus Jimenez could strew around, without even trying.

"They also fart a lot," continued Jesus, warming up to a bored audience. "You know why, don't you?" No one answered. His outrageous notions needed little encouragement.

"Y'know how they aspirate quickly with that kind'a reverse hissing sound, just before saying: *'Ah, soo desu ka?'* Well, they've gott'a get all that air outt'a their system. What better way than to cut loose?"

We still refused to laugh at his intellectual dandruff, sensing the blizzard in store, if only half provoked. But there was no stopping him now. He was on the roll, his notions growing woollier by the moment.

"You guys ever notice how Japs walk around with mouthfuls of crowned teeth? Pretty odd, wouldn't you say? Notice how some of 'em favor gold crowns, others stainless steel? Wanna know why?"

He paused for effect. Detecting none, he proceeded. "It's really a question of status with them. Gold's a noble metal, see. It's smoother on the tongue. Allows those wearing it to speak in Kanji, which is merely high class Ainu. Kind'a like Castilian to Spaniards, you know. That's why they both lisp a little. The ones wearing steel crowns are just plain oafs. The iron oxide makes 'em kind'a tongue-tied. They're lucky they can talk at all. That's why they can only speak in plain, ordinary Katakana!"

"You're more full of sod than a Christmas turkey!" despaired Lawson. Jesus Jimenez laughed heartily; Lawson had finally risen to the bait.

Cleanliness and godliness may not have been close neighbors in Japanese culture, but they sure loved warm baths. Neither shy nor retiring about their ablutions, a platoon of soldiers would line up in the middle of the street, every evening after supper. They'd prop up their rifles nearby, wigwam style, strip down to their bare essentials, and wait their turn to climb into a water-filled drum sitting over a low burning fire.

"That jerk at the end of the line must come out dirtier than when he went in," commented Lawson wryly, bemused by the daily open-air bathing ritual.

Laughing at his remark, I noticed the mangled remains of a giant toad that had been overrun by a vehicle, nearby. Imported from Australia just before the war, the ugly, outsized saps had infested the islands, generally making a nuisance of themselves.

"Let's add to his hygienic problems," I proposed, perversely associating the dead toad with the bathwater. We planned the operation carefully because it entailed some risk and meant using our last firecracker.

Deep in conversation, the disrobed troops failed to notice Lawson's approach. He had inched up on them on a dark alley, whose opposite end spilled unto the park, and safety. Crouching in the shadows, only a few yards away from the steaming drum, Lawson waited for me and Lobo to approach, on our purportedly innocent afternoon walk. Just as we came into view, he lit the firecracker, set it on the ground and scurried back to the park, with deliberate speed.

The timing was perfect. The hammerhead firecracker went off in the alley like a clap of thunder, the narrow walls echoing the thunderous report. Believing they were under attack, the naked troops scampered to retrieve their rifles, and then scattered frantically in all directions, ducking for cover. Taking advantage of all the commotion, I slowly and deliberately ambled past the abandoned drum, dropped the saucer-sized sap into it, and walked on, nonchalantly.

The startled soldiers looked ridiculous, guns at the ready and still stark naked. Recovering from their initial start, they returned to their drum apprehensively, only to spot the mangled toad floating on the filmy water. Sensing they'd been had, they started shouting after me.

"*Koko e kite!*" they ordered, commanding me to come back.

"*Wakarimasen,*" I answered limply, without stopping, pretending I hadn't understood the command. Lobo and I turned the corner and made tracks for the park and concealment in its bushes.

9. THE LAST HUDDLE

"I'm getting pretty sick of this corn porridge," muttered Luis, pushing the gruel around his saucer with his spoon. He was smart to wait till Mom and Dad had left the breakfast table before voicing his complaint.

"Yeah, me too" agreed Lawson." Thank God for the weevils in it, though. May be the only protein we're getting these days."

Life had grown grimmer as the war ground on. The siege had started to take its toll. People were looking gaunter, hollower eyed, like inmates in a concentration camp. Tuberculosis, the dread disease of the day, had become a constant worry. Our diet was down to Mongo beans, corn and rice. The servants threshed the rice so efficiently that they pounded the inner brown sheath right out of it, unwittingly depriving us of our only source of Vitamin B available those days. Vitamin deficiency made it even tougher to cure infections like *Bakukang*, a tropical skin condition that festered for months and had to be cauterized, because that was years before penicillin.

Clothing was also beginning to be a problem. Last imported from the States three years earlier, garments were starting to look increasingly ratty and threadbare. Mom would spend her days knitting T-shirts for us, using cotton twine originally meant for sewing sugar sacks. She and Mrs. Arana would sit side by side, knitting away, reminiscing on the good old days. If Mom worried about survival, she didn't show it. That was Dad's domain and he, as always, remained unshaken. He had stopped wearing tropical linen suits long ago, and now wore shorts and Mom's knitted T-shirts, like everyone else. He may have missed his golf and his tennis but there were other more pressing concerns, like survival, facing him now.

More out of habit than sustenance, Angel, the cook, still went to market every day, but now pushed a wheelbarrow brimming with large denomination, but increasingly worthless Japanese-issue bank notes. It wasn't long before the exchange of legal tender ceased altogether and all economic transactions reverted to the barter system. But even that primitive means of mercantile exchange was short-lived because people soon ran out of valuables and bed sheets and clothes to trade with.

And then, amidst the gloom of threatened existence, when spirits flagged and hope ebbed to its lowest, it happened; the Americans landed in the Philippines. MacArthur, who had left the islands in some haste three and a half years earlier, returned, as promised. It was like a prophecy fulfilled. From the edge of pain, the scent of freedom rose, faintly at first, then growing headier until it was, soon, impossible to quell.

"Hope they keep sweeping west and liberate us quickly," Dad kept repeating. The landing had taken place in Leyte, in the central Visayan group, a mere four islands east of ours.

The tempo of hostilities increased perceptively. Air raids were now a daily occurrence. The guerrillas in the outskirts of town had grown friskier. Iloilo was soon surrounded by several thousand, heavily armed guerrillas, with battle lines drawn no more than ten miles away. The trigger-happy band would redden the night sky with tracer bullets. Every day, at dawn, Japanese trucks rumbled back from the battlefield, laden with captured American arms. The siege soon degenerated into a standoff.

"These guerrillas are a bit of a joke," I commented at the dinner table, one evening. "All they seem do is ruddy up the night sky, just wasting ammunition!"

"Remember," remarked Dad, "the word 'guerrillas' stands for 'little wars'. Only people with faint hearts engage in them." I'll never forget that comment; it sounded so profound.

With airbases now only a spitting distance away, Flying Fortresses soon started flying missions over our island, dropping much larger bomb loads than had the earlier carrier airplanes. The large bombers disgorged their hefty 5OO-pounders on the Jaro airfield north or town and, occasionally, on the ships anchored in the Iloilo River, nearby. The detonations whitened in the mind, leaching away all humbug of bravery. But the sense that all this was but a prelude to invasion made their numbing roar and rending blasts strangely bearable, even oddly welcome.

Huddling in the shelter, we'd cup our ears with our hands, opening wide our mouths to prevent the air blast from rupturing eardrums. Large chunks of molten shrapnel and unspent bullets rained down on the patio outside. A direct hit on one of the ships docked on the nearby wharf once hurled its anchor clear over to our house. Crashing through the roof and smashing through two stories, the hot chunk of gnarled metal ended up only a few feet from the shelter, where we cringed in terror. I remember burning my fingers trying to pick it up, too soon after it landed.

The bombings intensified in November of 1944. The population was gripped by a mindless panic. Memories of an earlier invasion renewed the urge to huddle for safety. First in dribs and drabs, then in trickles, and finally in one mass exodus, the city's few remaining inhabitants flocked into San Agustin. Over four hundred people managed to cram themselves into its musty classrooms and auditoriums, refectories and empty monks' cells. Teeming with humanity, the Boy's School started to look like an overcrowded zoo.

We were assigned a cell that had once belonged to Fr. McCarthy, the American Chemistry teacher who'd been hustled to concentration camp, with the rest of the Allied citizenry when the war started. All five of us were jammed into the friar's cozy 13 by 30-foot cell. The servants shrewdly elected to remain at home.

"Claustrophobia," Lawson reminded us at dinner, the first evening, "is the fear of cloisters." He must have picked up that nugget of wisdom from Jesus Jimenez, who was always parroting his older brothers' factoids.

"You should have as much room in heaven!" countered Mom, huffily.

"I'm not so sure I wanna go there if it's gonna be this crowded," I countered, siding with Lawson. Mom pretended shock at the heretical remark but held her peace; she knew I was only joking. We were almost fifteen and starting to feel our oats.

Life in San Agustin was a little like living in a concentration camp, only without the barbed wire. With so many kids living under the same roof, hardly a day went by without some breech of conduct. A favorite pastime was dropping in, uninvited, on the Indians' quarters, trying to get a closer whiff of the delightful smells of cooking *tanduri* pork and curry chicken wafting out of their compound. Rubbing our tummies, we'd demonstrate approval with what we thought were Indian-sounding phrases like "*nam nam*," hoping that flattery would earn us a nibble. It never worked. The battle-scarred cook invariably shooed us away with her ladle and a string of Hindi oaths.

"Nice old dear!" muttered Lawson, scampering out of harm's way. We tried it, over and over again, with diminishing success.

'Peeping Tom-ing' was an equally unrewarding pastime. When darkness fell, we'd maraud around the compound, sneaking peeks at disrobing refugees. Much to our chagrin, only aging, overweight women would leave their blinds up, so that the episodes never figured greatly in our Confessions, when Saturdays rolled around.

Not that penance would have been that severe; we always made sure to avoid the Spanish friars, flocking, instead, to Fr. Henry, the aging Irish chaplain of the nearby Hospital San Pablo, who was as conveniently deaf as the Blarney stone, and understood about as much Spanish.

There were other interesting but less titillating distractions. Spider fights became one of our favorites. We'd hunt for different varieties in the surrounding bushes, stashing the insects away in empty matchboxes until fight time. We'd then fish them out, lay them on opposite ends of a stripped palm leaf rib and gently coax the hairy contenders toward each other.

The spiders approached warily, each with their unique fighting stance. The red *Pulahan* tried to wrap its opponent with the sticky silk it drew, with blinding speed, out of its rear end. The 'King' variety, on the other hand, was a smallish, pincer-armed white spider that prevailed by injecting its paralyzing venom into the enemy's exposed legs or underbelly. The live spoils were carefully tucked away into the victor's matchbox, there to serve as its week's nutrition.

Chess became the rage for a while. Luis became an accomplished player, beating everybody in sight, including Paco Perez, the aging doyen and local champion, especially when the old coot was in his cups, which he often was.

When we ran out of distractions, we'd go watch Japanese soldiers at their bayonet practice, in the fields where we had once played soccer. Their frenzied *Banzai's* sent shivers up and down my spine.

"The beggars could use those on us one day," commented Lawson morbidly. The dreadful thought brought back memories of Iru. I never went back to watch them bayonet practice again, after that.

When all else failed, we'd go back to marbles. Ives Partier gave birth to a hookworm in the middle of a marbles game, one day. Unbeknownst to him, he'd been carrying it for months and had grown increasingly pale from sharing his meager essence with the disgusting parasite. It was his turn to shoot when, suddenly, he started coughing and gagging violently. Transfixed, we watched a white, three foot long worm wriggle out of his nose and into the bright sunlight. Kurt, who had withered to a fifty-pound weakling, started putting on a little weight after the 'accouchement', as Jesus Jimenez fondly called the delivery.

American bombers redoubled their bombing raids, knowing that the civilian population was safely tucked away in San Agustin. Uncomfortable about being sitting-duck targets, the Japanese, one day, decided to order us all back to our homes, there to resume our proper hostage roles.

As the crowd shuffled out of the chapel after Mass one Sunday morning, Uyeki turned up with four of his Kempitai goons, to announce that we had to return to our homes. The hubbub that rose from the stunned crowd was promptly quelled by Uyeki.

"You will evacuate premises in twenty four hours! Order of Imperial Japanese Army!" he bellowed, hand ominously resting on his holstered gun.

And that was the end of that. There was no room for further discussion or dissent.

Spotting me as I emerged from the chapel with Luis and Lawson, Uyeki swaggered over to us, rudely shoving people aside in his wake. I noticed that he'd grown visibly older. His bespectacled eyes came to rest on Lawson, ogling him with the unfocused stare of someone observing a mirage. A splinter of hardness crossed his eyes, old suspicions flashing briefly across his hardened features.

"You not really Spanish," he blurted out, staring darkly at Lawson.

We all froze.

"I am so, too!" responded the Scot without even batting an eyelid.

The Spanish accent we had tried so hard to overlay on his distinctive Scottish brogue disappeared in the heat of battle, when he needed it most. Deep under my panic, I felt a surge of pride for him and his gutsiness, standing there, facing the enemy, like the young Bruce himself, at Bannockburn.

"I told you before we're Basque," I volunteered weakly. "We just look different. Look at my other brother here. He's just as fair haired and blue eyed. He also talks kind'a funny, see?" I said, prodding Luis, hoping he'd step into the breach.

"Oo-oo," said Luis with an eerie, hooting sound, curling his lips and crossing his eyes at Uyeki, like someone demented. Uyeki didn't buy the distraction. He kept staring at Lawson's sandy hair and pale blue eyes, and then at Luis'.

The Scot's were fairer and his freckles unmistakably Saxon. Mercifully, one of his Japanese cohorts whispered in Uyeki's ear something about the crowd getting restive, that it was time to leave.

"I come check papers one of these days," he warned ominously, frowning at us as he strutted out of the building, a sorry caricature of the Samurai he was so desperately trying to emulate.

"We've gotta stop making this sod lose face," whispered Lawson a bit shaken by the encounter. "It sure looks like the gig's up though, doesn't it?" he added apprehensively.

"Don't worry," I said, drawing him away from the curious crowd that was now starting to mill around us, trying to find out what the exchange had been all about. "I've got a plan," I whispered, as I led him out of the hallway. "I'll tell you about it later. Let's go."

Dad caught up with us shortly after. After relating the events to him, he assured Lawson that everything was going to be alright, that his citizenship papers were in order, and that they'd been approved long ago and had the proper seal of the Spanish Legation in Manila.

But the evil look on Uyeki's face and the menace in his voice were not easily dispelled. Deep down, Lawson and I knew that there would be trouble ahead.

We packed our belongings that evening, and vacated San Agustin before noon the next day. The exodus reminded me of one of those old News-Around-The-World shorts, where Chinese refugees were seen dragging their carts teetering with worldly belongings, escaping the Japanese armies advancing on Nanking, or somewhere.

Lawson seemed listless and out of sorts the day of the move. Luis and I tried to cheer him up but he remained dispirited. Late that night, while everyone slept, he and I slipped out into the upstairs patio, just outside our bedroom. We leaned silently on the moonlit balustrade for a long time, each wrapped in his own thoughts.

"The noose is really tightening, isn't it," he whispered after a while. "I don't think Dad's papers are gonna hold up under scrutiny. After all, I was British when the war started, remember?" he reflected, almost plaintively. There was something disturbing about the logic. Lawson had always had an uncanny knack for going to the jugular of things.

"That's what it looks like to me, too," I agreed, hopelessly, having shared the nagging thought. "We've got to get out of here before Uyeki comes and gets you," I said.

"We can't just break through the guerrilla lines and head for the hills," he said. "That'd be crazy. We'd stop a few stray bullets before we walked two paces into no-man's-land."

"I think there's another way out. I've been thinking about it a lot."

"What's that?"

"Guimarás!"

The thought had lain in the back of my mind all those many months, quiet under the taut wire of conscious thought, like a dim flicker, visible only through side vision. And then, suddenly, breaking forth into the open ragged field of consciousness, it became eminent good sense.

Mention of the magic island struck Lawson like a thunderclap, leaving him speechless, as if under a spell.

"Gorblime!" he said finally, smacking his forehead with the palm of his hand. "Why didn't I think of that myself?"

The long, pent-up dream of freedom gradually took shape in our minds' eye. The realization that adventure was the door to it made its lightness even headier. Freedom awaited across the narrow straits, where the green mountains of the emerald isle had beckoned for years.

We'd studied the tides that had quarreled with the Sea Hawk on our brief excursions to nearby beaches, and had watched the big *paraos* sail gracefully to and from the small green island that lay to the southeast, no more than three miles away. Over the years, we had struck up enough conversations with *parao* sailors to know that they were a friendly lot, that their little island was hilly, with lots of rivers and plenty of fish and fowl, which they peddled in our marketplace. We could live off of that, easily.

The time had finally come to answer the island's clear call.

10. ESCAPE

The fear of impending capture lent a certain urgency to our preparations. Only Luis knew about our plans. He wanted to come along with us but the Sea Hawk was barely large enough for two. Our baggage had to be light because the boat's water line was already riding dangerously high, even without the added ballast. A slingshot and a pocket knife, some matches, twine, a couple of rusty fishhooks and some band-aids made up our survival kit. Two cotton sweaters and a few bananas wrapped in a mosquito net completed our Spartan baggage.

The night before we sailed, I wrote my parents a short note by the light of a kerosene lamp.

Dear Mom and Dad,

Lawson and I are sailing for Guimarás at dawn tomorrow. By the time you get this letter we'll already be there. We know it's only a matter of time before Uyeki comes looking for Lawson. He won't find us waiting for him. Lawson says he'd rather suffer hardship out in the open than in concentration camp.

> *Don't worry about us. We'll be O.K. We'll be back*
> *as soon as the heat's off. Lawson says to keep a stiff*
> *upper lip.*
>
> *Love,*
> *José Mari*

I knew that Mom would be worried sick and cry rivers over that note, but felt that Dad would see beyond the initial surprise and realize, perhaps even with a little twinge of pride, that his children were only doing what came naturally. He had, after all, done the same thing in his youth, when he left his Pyrenees as a young man and sailed off into the unknown.

I gave the note to Luis. He was sorry he couldn't join us, but he understood.

"You guys take care," he said. I thought I detected a note of concern in his voice as he bade us farewell.

"Hold the fort down, kid. We'll be back before you know it," I said, trying to cheer him up.

We got up long before dawn the next morning and snuck out of the house, unnoticed except by Lobo, who wagged his tail in brief acknowledgement, and then went back to sleep.

The road to the beach was deserted. We dragged the Sea Hawk from its lean-to behind the dunes, all the way to the water's edge. A dozing seagull stirred into flight, croaking its displeasure with wild and vacant calls.

In their convent overlooking the beach, the nuns from the Sagrado Corazón were already singing their Matins. Lawson fell silent, wrapped in thoughts of old hurts and healing hands.

"Florence Nightingale could'a learned a few tricks from my little Sisters," he whispered. I was always touched by the way he used the possessive, every time he talked about his religious friends.

Backlit by the rising sun, a solitary cloud wandered, innocent and lofty in the vacant sky above. Licking a finger, I raised it in a maritime manner, sensing the direction of the wind on it.

"Let's go," I said. "It's time."

Tying our knapsack to the base of the mast, we manhandled the Sea Hawk into the crystal quiet sea and shoved off, paddling to get a lead on the southerly-flowing current.

"I feel a hint of a Northwesterly," commented Lawson a short while later. "We won't have to tack much with it."

"We'll need all the help we can get to fight this tide," I said. "It could easily sweep us down the strait and into the open seas, probably all the way to Mindanao. That's a few hundred miles to the south."

Paddling vigorously, we cleared the breakwater and were on our way. A brush of wind whispered more strongly in the channel. Gingerly, we raised the rig to half mast, trying to get a feel for its tug. Gaining confidence, we raised it all the way up, letting out the rest of the sail. We watched it billow joyously, as we listened to the rigging's hums and whistles. The Sea Hawk sniffed into the wind and ran with the tide, sailing grandly toward the dark green hump of Guimarás.

We sailed in silence for a while, glad to be where the world could not intrude. The wet sound of the bow crest filled me with jumbled emotions of power and danger. I didn't know exactly what it was that I loved about the sea; probably its absence of roads and its wind trails to nowhere. Perhaps, they were just dim recollections of some ancient Basque mariner in me.

We sailed for about an hour, at no more than two or three knots, and were soon past the point of no return. Guimarás sat proudly on the magical sea, thrusting ever stronger and higher as we got closer. Its forests and rocky outcroppings slowly took on distinct shapes and contours. Dead reckoning told me that the tide at mid strait was tugging at us more strongly than the wind was blowing us towards land.

"Let's take a harder tack," I proposed. "Guimarás is slipping by too fast."

We started taking in more water with the new bearing.

"We'd better slack off on this tack just a wee bit," said Lawson with some alarm. "We're about to get swamped."

"Let's maintain course," I said with the conviction that danger sometimes lends. "I'd sure hate to end up in Mindanao. Let's just bail a little faster." We bailed out the overflow as fast as we could with the two coconut shells we'd brought along for just that purpose. It was hard work but it seemed to be working.

We'd been sailing for about three hours when we finally glided past the jutting cape that harbored the coastal village we could see from Iloilo, on a clear day. The tide seemed to slacken a bit after sailing past the small cape. The harsh wind died down to a whisper just as we got to leeward of the hulking mountain range running along the western length of the island.

The rugged hills directly above us grew gradually more abrupt. We could now discern whitewater streams spilling down the mountainside and into the sea. A little farther on, the coastline jutted out slightly westward, as if to greet us. We could now clearly see the waves slamming against the rocks, mindlessly going back for more punishment.

Suddenly, there was no more land farther south. There, along the slit of the horizon, the green sea touched nothing but blue sky. We knew we had to make landfall soon, or be swept past the southern tip of the island, now no more than half a mile away. Paddling furiously, we eased the Sea Hawk out of the swing of the sea and into the flat shallows of a mangrove swamp. Water fowl stirred among the branches and flew off into the humid air, skimming over the green, marshy waters before soaring into awkward flight.

It was past noon. We were thirsty and exhausted but elated with our feat. It could have easily turned into a disaster. I almost felt like kneeling and kissing the ground in thanksgiving, as in those storybook pictures of Conquistadors landing on desolate Caribbean beaches. But the muck we were standing on did not invite drama. A silent prayer of thanksgiving would have to do.

Dragging the boat onto dry land, we covered it with dry palm leaves. We knew we'd never use it again, but there was no need giving away any clues to the Japanese, should they come sniffing around for us. Out of the bed sheet sail we fashioned a knapsack, stuffing our meager belongings into it.

We turned to look at the camouflaged boat one last time.

"I hate to just leave it there," said Lawson sentimentally. "She sure stood us in good stead."

"Don't worry. We'll build another one when we go back." I paused before adding: "Wonder if it'll be as good as the Sea Hawk, though," I mused.

We stood there for a moment, almost at stark attention, moved by the pathos of the moment, looking at the gallant ship for the last time.

"Come on, let's check out the land of the Lotus Eaters," I said, striking off toward the hills.

There was no trail at first, just an absence of undergrowth along gradually ascending foothills. A mountain range lay before us, like a crooked backbone shoved along the western half of the narrow island, its rocky outcroppings occasionally punching through lush forests.

Instinct warned us to avoid human contact until we could get a feel of the land. Our greatest worry was running into the Japanese in the island. We weren't too sure about the reception we'd get from the natives, either. But right then, water was our first priority. Parched by the sun and caked with sea salt, our lips thirsted for drink.

Winding our way uphill, we spotted a small fishing village far below us, crammed against the foot of the hill we were climbing. It was the village we had sailed past earlier, the same one we could see across the strait from Iloilo, on a clear day. We stuck to the highlands, with their promise of solitude and anonymity. We'd find sanctuary in its forests. Its streams and wildlife would provide all the food we would need.

A narrow footpath soon materialized, leading sharply up the mountain. Thick stands of Lauan trees provided a canopy that hid the mild November sun from view for long stretches of trail at a time. The rocky path wandered through the dark forest, flanked by tree trunks writhing confusedly up for light.

Suddenly, there was a glint of water against the dark background of the woods. We came upon a little stream that tumbled and flashed down the hill across our path. After quenching our thirst in its cool, sun-speckled waters, we stripped down and splashed about in them, all cares forgotten. Memories of Igbarás came flitting back with whims of simpler, more innocent days. Climbing out of the brook we stretched out in the sun to dry, blissfully munching on the bananas we'd brought along. It was good to be alive, awake and young to adventure.

We soon resumed the uphill hike. The steep climb was broken by an occasional dale, where natives had carved a clearing out of the forest, for truck and tobacco farming. Steering clear of the plots, we stuck to the woods to avoid any premature confrontation with skittish, possibly even hostile natives. The occasional parrot screech or sounds of scurrying lemurs in the underbrush startled us at first. Iguanas pierced the silence of the forest with their rhythmic, territorial 'to-ko' calls.

"The natives claim an iguana's grip is so powerful you couldn't pull it off if one of them ever landed on you," I said, quoting a snippet of Eusebio's dubious jungle lore.

"Get off it!" responded Lawson, incredulous.

"No, really! They say the only way to pry it loose is to place a mirror next to it. It thinks another iguana is threatening it, so it jumps off of you and onto the mirror," I explained, unconvinced of the improbable story, myself.

"Pure poppycock!" said Lawson skeptically. "Speaking of mirrors," he rejoined, "do you know they're great for fishing? All you need is a small one and a banana."

"How'd that work?" I asked warily, sensing a Jesus Jimenez 'gotcha!' in the offing.

"Well, first you stick a little mirror below the water's surface. Fish are pretty vain fellows, you see, so they'll come look at themselves for hours on end. Then, when they least expect it, you jerk the mirror out of the water. They'll jump right out of the surface, trying to follow their image. All you gotta do then is take the banana, plug the hole with it and pick up the little bleeder."

His raucous, thigh-slapping laughter awoke a dozing hornbill in the canopy above us, startling it into flight.

"That's not half as clever as hunting elephants with a pair of binoculars and a toothpick," I countered, warming up to the occasion.

"Well?" he asked, bracing himself.

"First, you spot an elephant through the wrong end of the binoculars. It's so teensy, all you gotta do is reach out, stick it with the toothpick and stuff it in your pocket."

"Hunger's making you daffy," he said, trying to disguise a smile. The mere mention of hunger made me suddenly conscious of a gnawing sensation at the pit of my stomach.

"It'll be a while before we eat again unless we hunt something before it gets too dark," I said.

It was now getting on six o'clock. We'd been climbing for several hours and were growing increasingly exhausted. We'd been on the lookout for mountain fowl or birds to bring down with our slingshots, but it was hard to concentrate on hunting while grunting up the rock-strewn trail.

Suddenly, we heard voices in the distance. Someone was walking down the narrow trail, heading our way. Jumping off the trail, we took cover behind the thick underbrush. As the voices drew nearer, we were relieved that they were not speaking Japanese. Soon, two farmers loomed through the bashful *hiyâ-hiyâ* ferns in front of us, walking so close past us that we could have reached out and touched them. The two men ambled past, oblivious of our presence. We waited until we could no longer hear them before getting back on the trail to resume our uphill trek.

113

"Come to think of it," I commented to Lawson when we were well beyond earshot, "it wouldn't make sense for them to have been Japanese. They need all the troops they can muster in Iloilo, surrounded as they are. Not even the Japanese Empire has enough soldiers to garrison every one of this country's seven thousand islands!"

"You're right!" said Lawson, relieved by the thought. "But there's nothing to keep them from sending a platoon of goons after us if that Uyeki friend of yours ever gets the urge, is there?"

"He's no friend of mine," I answered testily. "Besides, we'll see them coming if they do. That's one nice thing about heights. Terrain advantage, you know."

"You've been reading too many of those Tom Swift books. They're making you a bit barmy."

I smiled at his funny turns of phrase, though I didn't understand them half the time. I sometimes suspected he just made them up as he went.

The steep trail leveled off, half a mile farther uphill. There, before us, in the middle of a small clearing, stood an abandoned nipa hut. Pale smoke drifted up from its chimney, dispersed by the shafts of receding sunlight that pierced the dark Lauan overhang.

We approached the hut warily. Sensing no sounds of life inside, we climbed the rickety ladder and cautiously entered the solitary room. There was no one inside the sparsely furnished habitation. Walking over to the kitchen area, we found a large blackened pot resting on three large stones straddling a bed of still warm embers. The two farmers we'd seen earlier must have just had supper there and hadn't bothered cleaning up their leftovers.

We set to with our fingers and ate the white sticky rice avidly, using our fingernails to scrape the last burnt *ducút* off the bottom of the pot. We helped ourselves to a few bruised bananas lying on the window sill, and finished the water in a half empty bamboo container that hung from the wall.

It was dark outside when we finished our meager meal. The uncharacteristic cool of the evening reminded me a little of Baguio, the town perched in the mountain uplands of Luzon, where we used to spend our summers before the war.

We found a rolled *petate* mat propped up in a corner of the room. Spreading it out over the yielding bamboo floor, we strung up our mosquito net over it and crawled in. The gauzy spread of the Milky Way cut a swath of light across the sky outside the open window. An early moon hung limply over us, soaking the quiet forest with its silver balm. We were bone weary but pleased with the way things were turning out. All in all, it had been a day to be proud of.

"I guess they've read my note by now," I reflected. I was starting to feel sorry for Mom. "Surely they'll understand, don't you think?"

"I think Dad will," answered Lawson philosophically. "I'm not so sure about Mom, though," he added. "She's probably worried sick about us being eaten up by some Boa Constrictor or something equally dreadful."

Jose Maria Lacambra

"I know she's praying double time," I agreed. I could just
see her worrying her rosary beads, shiny now from years of
prayer. "The meek shall inherit the earth," I thought out
loud, thinking of her.

"You know, I never understood that prattle in Sunday
school," commented Lawson, curling up in his corner of
the mat. "I mean, the meek have been run over for donkey's
years around here. And the blokes who give the other cheek
always seem to get bopped twice, don't they?"

"Well it wouldn't be much of a religion if they just asked
you to do what comes naturally and just had a merry old
time, would it?" I caught myself smiling in the dark. The
pious statement reminded me of one of Father Budul's less
inspired commentaries.

"I guess you're right," mulled Lawson. "And there wouldn't
be people like nuns to care for the sick, either," he added
wistfully.

A long silence followed. I could sense the old hurts flooding
over him.

"I know it sounds kind'a corny, but thanks for everything,"
he said.

"Why?" I asked, a little embarrassed.

"Just because."

I remembered how the inadequate answer used to infuriate
me, when we were kids. Now it didn't matter. After a long,

116

pregnant silence, he added: "I'd like for you to come visit me in Scotland, when this is all over."

"Yeah," I answered sleepily. "I'd sure like to check out those misty moors."

We both started laughing.

Years earlier, Lawson's brothers had written from their boarding school in Scotland, describing the land's foul weather and misty moors. I knew that, back in the Dark Ages, the French had stopped the Moors in a town called Poitiers, and questioned Lawson's brothers sighting any of the North Africans all the way up in Scotland. My having confused moors for Moors had thrown Lawson off, but only momentarily. Drawing from some ingrained tribal wisdom, he weighed into the garbled discussion.

"The French couldn't wallop anybody, even if they tried! They were probably just mucking about, as usual," he had answered huffily. "Moors are pretty misty characters, anyway. My brothers say so in their letter, don't they? It couldn't ha' been that hard to give the Frogs the slip and keep on going all the way up to Scotland, would it?"

"We used to have some great arguments when we were kids, didn't we," mused Lawson, half asleep now.

"Yeah. I'd paint you into some corner and you'd answer 'Just because!' I hated it when you said that."

We laughed ourselves to sleep.

11. GUIMARÁS

The loud squawks of cockatoos woke us up the next morning. Sunlight was streaming in through the open window as the day expanded. Outside, lazy patches of mist loitered on the early meadow. We slipped out of the hut to hunt for breakfast. The outcome was never in doubt; years of practice had honed our slingshot skills, and it was to pay off now. Half an hour later we were watching three skewered sparrows and a hornbill roasting over the embers.

"One can certainly live off the land like this indefinitely," I commented, tearing into the slightly burnt meat. It was delicious.

"Sure beats corn porridge and weevils!" answered Lawson through a mouthful of chewy hornbill breast. For the first time in our lives, we were eating food that we ourselves had hunted and cooked. There was a deep sense of pride in the accomplishment.

"Let's keep climbing this mountain," suggested Lawson after breakfast. "We'll get a better view from the top."

The narrow footpath led northward, growing progressively steeper as we proceeded. At the end of the sharp ascent, we came upon a small hamlet hugging the side of a hill. Giving it a wide berth, we bushwhacked our way cross-country until we reached the southern ridges of the mountain we'd been guiding ourselves by, ever since we landed. We finally reached the top after one last push, and sat down to a well-deserved rest.

The view from the abrupt, windy crags was magnificent. It was a solitary kind of place, where the air was clean and free, and alive with sunshine. From somewhere, far below, the distant sound of the sea rose to greet us. To the west and across the strait, the sun-bright sea bullied the black sands of the Iloilo beaches, touching them with a lacework of spume. A little farther west lay what must have been the beaches of Arévalo and Otón.

"That must be Otón, over to the west of town," I said, shading my eyes against the glare of the noonday sun. Memories of fun-filled Sundays spent there came flooding over me. "We sure had some good times at the Jimenez' beach house there."

"Yeah," said Lawson. "Remember those pitched battles we used to have on the water with mangoes?"

"Yeah, when there weren't any jellyfish around. I remember looking up at these very mountains we're sitting on, from that very beach, wondering what it was like to be up here," I said. "And now here we are!"

119

Iloilo looked unfamiliar, seen from our new perspective. I was surprised to see that its broad, meandering river literally sliced the town in half.

"I never realized the town laid out East to West, like that. Not even when Dad and I used to fly over it, years ago, in that little Stimson eight-seater." Dad sometimes took me along with him on his inspection tours to the different sugar plantations around the western Visayan Islands.

"It's a pretty large town, isn't it," commented Lawson. Over a hundred thousand people had once inhabited the sprawling city.

"You can really see the scars of war on it now," I said. "There're whole sections of it kind'a smudged and lifeless."

"Yeah, and there's no traffic in the streets. It's like a ghost town now, isn't it," remarked Lawson.

"I think I see our house!" I said, taking my bearings from the patch of green that had to be Plaza Libertad.

"Where?" asked Lawson, peering at the distant network of streets.

"See that second hook in the river? See the large house occupying the whole block, just south of it? I think that's it!"

"Gorblime! I believe you're right!" said Lawson. "I wonder if they're missing us much down there."

"I know Mom is. Let's see, today's Sunday and it's about noon, right? See that white belfry overlooking the big green square? That's San Jose. She's probably in that church this very minute." It seemed strange to be able to tell where someone was, from so far away.

"She's probably praying for us to her Virgin of Roncesvalles," I added. "I loved to hear her stories about Roland, the noble knight, and how he got beaten by the Basques in the mountains near her home. I can't wait to go there and ski in winter. And Dad's town near there, where young men run with the brave bulls in the streets, just for the fun of it. Boy, have I got a lot of catching up to do when this war's over!"

"Strange bunch, those Basques," ventured Lawson. "Why would anybody want to be gored by bulls?"

"It's the challenge, that's why. Why do people climb mountains and sail uncharted seas? Didn't I tell you Basques were great sailors?"

"Not as good as the British," he taunted.

"Oh yeah?" I answered, rising to the bait. "A Basque named Elcano beat Drake around the world," I said smugly. "Beat him to the punch by half a century, too!"

"Yeah. You told me," said Lawson, weary of my breast-beating. "Hey, do you hear what I hear?" The sound of airplanes became suddenly audible.

"They're American!" I said.

Over the past few months we'd learned to distinguish between the sound of American and Japanese airplane engines; the Americans' hummed, the Japanese wheezed and coughed. The difference in quality between the U.S. and the Made-in-Japan toys that Luis and I used to play with years earlier, still seemed to persist, even with these newer, deadlier toys.

A dozen P-47 Thunderbolts came into view moments later. Flying a lazy V-formation in the vacant sky, they gradually gained height before peeling off, one by one, swooping down on the city in front of us. It was a grandstand view of the kind of attack I usually watched from the receiving end. Before pulling up, the planes disgorged dark oblong objects which tumbled lazily onto a building complex sprawling in a large meadow, on the western edge of town. Suddenly, bright flashes began to light up the group of buildings in what appeared to be a series of direct hits.

Shortly after, the sound of bombs carried to us, like grunts of puny thunder riding the broad back of the wind. The planes made several strafing passes at the boats docked on the river before breaking off the attack and flying off in the direction whence they came. Tongues of flame licked at the wounded complex, black smoke billowing thousands of feet above it. We sat there, speechless, eyes glued to the fiery spectacle before us.

"It's like watching one of those Fox Movietone shorts, isn't it," I commented, mesmerized by the fire.

"Right from first row in balcony," answered Lawson. "I wonder what those burning buildings are," he added.

"That's about where San Agustin is, isn't it?" I said. "Surely they wouldn't bomb our school!"

"You can never tell," said Lawson. "The Japs may have moved in after we moved out. Sneaky buggers!"

The planes were returning to their base. They were now over the big island of Negros, a dozen miles to the East of us, heading straight for the eight thousand foot Mt. Kanlaón volcano which rose majestically, to meet them on even terms.

"I remember how Dad used to take me along to the La Carlota sugar plantation, at the foot of that volcano right there," I commented. "I rode my first horse there."

"La Carlota, wasn't that where that daffy Mr. Kauffman used to live?"

"Yup! Fritz Kauffman. British like you, despite the name. He was the sugar Central's Manager there. Loony as a fruitcake! Once sailed into Manila on a P & O liner, disguised as an Indian Maharajah. Big government reception and everything aboard the liner, waiting for him. Fooled 'em all. Even had his picture on the papers the next day, blackened face, turban and all."

"You're kidding! How'd he get away with it?"

"Just disappeared into thin air. Snookered 'em all!"

Our height had given us a better perspective of Guimarás. The island was about twenty miles long and less than five, at

123

its widest. A few hamlets dotted both slopes of the mountain range on whose ridge we stood. A fairly large barrio squatted at the base of the eastern foothills, hard by the sea. Judging from the many *paraos* dotting its beaches and sailing the wrinkled sea around it, the village's inhabitants must have all been fishermen.

"I can't spot any launches like the ones the Japanese moor along the Iloilo River," commented Lawson. "Probably there really aren't any Japs on this island, after all. Maybe it's safe to check out one of those towns down there."

"I don't see any rush. We've got all the food we need up here. Besides, you know they'll never find us here. Let's just hang around for a while."

"Well, it's a little like playing 'hide and go seek' and being 'it' all the time. Gets kind'a old after a while," said Lawson, moodily.

"You're not getting tired already, are you?" I chided. "We just got here! We should hide out a while. Then we can check out one of those small barrios down there. Kind'a feel these people out. Remember, we're foreigners to them and about as useful as tits on a bull."

Lawson chuckled at the anatomical oddity. "I guess you're right. Let's just follow this ridge here a wee bit farther. I wanna see what's in the northern tip of this island, nearer Iloilo. We may see tomorrow's bombing from ringside," he suggested.

We slogged our way northward, along the abrupt ridge. We found ourselves taking more frequent rests as we trudged the rock-strewn path, finding the going increasingly rough on our sore feet.

"I wonder how long it'll take before we wear holes through these sneakers," I commented on one of our rest stops.

"My toes are almost showing through already," said Lawson. "We'll just have to go native, that's all. Filipinos think nothing of walking barefoot. We'll just have to grow calluses like them."

We descended a few hundred feet till we found what looked like an animal trail. We had noticed a gradual change in vegetation as we gained altitude. Majestic eucalyptus had replaced the mahogany of the lower elevations. The strong sweet smell pervading the forest was lung-cleansing. It reminded me a little of Baguio.

"I wonder how the Iturraldes are doing," I mused, as we sat down in a sunlit glen to catch our breath. "I bet Carmiña is pretty grown up by now. I sure took a shine to her in Igbarás. Puppy love, I think they call it."

The Iturraldes were friends of the family. They'd gone back to Manila after sharing our home in the hills of Igbarás, just before the Japanese invasion. They had a daughter, Carmiña, who was about my age. Something about her really turned me on.

"Becky Simmons did that to me, too," said Lawson. "Her folks were from some place called Inverness, in Scotland. They'd spend weekends with us in our beach house in Arévalo. She was a year older than me. Treated me like I was a baby all the time. I hated it. But I liked playing 'Doctor' with her. She was kind'a cute." He paused a moment before adding: "Wonder how she's doing in that concentration camp they sent them all to."

"You should write her a letter when we get back," I suggested. Lawson looked at me strange.

We resumed our walk in silence, the heavy breathing from the uphill climb discouraging any further conversation.

Suddenly, there was a deep-throated snorting sound nearby, followed by a rustle of leaves. Quick as lightning, a large black *jabalina* boar rushed out into the open, fangs slashing the air in a blur of ivory. Its trailing brood tarried behind in the safety of the underbrush, squealing encouragement at the charging sow.

"Quick! Grab a limb!" I shouted, scrambling up the trunk of the nearest tree. Lawson was just starting to clamber up a branch on the opposite side of the trail when the boar hit him on the leg.

"Yeow!" he cried out in a damaged way. Pulling himself up on a low limb, he managed to swing both legs out of reach of the sow's vicious fang thrusts. The bristling *jabalina* grunted and snorted ferociously for a few seconds and then broke off the attack, dashed back to its young and disappeared in the underbrush.

"How bad is it?" I called out, watching him looking down at his wounded leg.

"Just a nasty gash. Don't think any bone's broken," he answered weakly.

Jumping down from my tree limb, I ran over to help him down from his branch. A clean slit cut across his left calf. The gaping wound was starting to bleed a little.

"You're lucky. It doesn't look like any artery or vein got cut," I said, relieved at the relatively minor damage. "Think you can walk O.K.?" I asked, as I helped him hobble over to a rock, by the side of the trail.

"Yeah, I'm alright. I can manage."

"Let's just try hiking back down to that stream we crossed a while back. We'll wash the wound there and dress it. Just let it bleed a while. That'll get rid of any dirt that might have gotten in it."

Shaken, Lawson looked a little paler than usual. He limped down the path, holding on to my shoulder for support. Eventually, we got to the little stream, where I eased him down on a rock. Scooping up some water, I cleansed the gaping wound as best I could, fighting back nausea as I noticed the layers of fatty tissue jiggling under the skin. Deeper down, the white of exposed bone lay bare and motionless.

Tearing up a spare T-shirt into bandage strips, I wrapped the wound tightly to stop the bleeding.

"That should take care of it for a while," I said, pleased at my attempt at First Aid. "I think you'll be needing some stitches, though. Perhaps even a tetanus shot. There's bound to be a doctor in one of those villages down there. Even a nurse would do."

"Witch doctor, more likely," groused Lawson, skeptically. "I dread to think what that wild boar would have done to my guts if I'd fallen off that limb."

"Yeah, I'm glad you didn't. Let's try walking down this path here," I proposed, pointing to a descending fork in the faint trail. "Probably we'll find help before we get there. Here, why don't you lean on me."

"I'll be alright," he said bravely. Proceeding gingerly down the hill, we managed to make fairly good time, until Lawson's pain started to set in. Barely noticeable at first, his limp became increasingly apparent as the afternoon wore on. We were taking more frequent breaks now. A makeshift crutch which I whittled out of a sapling seemed to help some. We resumed our descent, occasionally slipping and sliding painfully down the leaf-strewn trail.

We talked little as we struggled, more slowly now, down switchbacks and nettled undergrowth. The dark was gaining on us. I sensed that we wouldn't make it down all the way to the barrio before nightfall. I started hoping that we'd come across some human habitation, where we could perhaps spend the night.

"What'll we tell these guys when they ask us who we are and what we're doing here?" asked Lawson, bemused by our predicament.

"This is one time when truth is going to sound stranger than fiction," I commented. "But I think they'll buy it. Who knows, they may even help us. It'd be nice if we could find Cirilo, that old chauffeur we used to have. He was from Guimarás, I think. I know he'd take care of us."

"Strange how chauffeurs turn out to be a cut above, isn't it?" said Lawson pensively. "Ours really saved my life. I wish I knew where he is now, so I could thank him properly."

That was more than he had ever said about his close call with death, three years earlier. He'd always been a little reluctant to talk about it. He must have felt guilty about surviving, while his parents hadn't made it.

"*Para dirá!*" a threatening voice suddenly boomed out of the darkening forest; someone was ordering us to halt. We stopped dead in our tracks. Startled by the command, we peered into the gloaming thicket, from where the voice had come.

There, barely visible, a man of shortish stature stood, dressed in what looked like a camouflage army uniform. He had a stubby, wicked-looking submachine gun leveled at us, and appeared to be as startled by our presence as we of his. He sized us up for a few moments, appearing increasingly puzzled by two European boys ambling along his primeval forest, miles from civilization.

"*Sinó kamó?*" he asked, demanding to know who we were. Unlike Igbarás, where a different dialect was spoken, neither the body of water nor the short distance separating the island from Iloilo were enough to alter the version of the Visayan dialect which Lawson and I spoke fluently.

"*Siá Canô; akó Cachilâ,*" I explained, trying to make it sound perfectly plausible that Lawson was American and that I was Spanish. I figured it'd be easier and more effective to change Lawson's nationality, knowing how much Filipinos liked Americans.

My flawless accent in his native tongue, complete with the local mannerism for the two foreign nationalities, only compounded the man's confusion. But I was relieved to notice that his submachine gun was now no longer pointed in our direction. In a tone less urgent, he proceeded with his interrogation, switching now to English.

"Where you prom?" he asked in the distinctive native accent. It had always puzzled me why Filipinos had the same trouble pronouncing their f's as the Japanese had with their l's, the Chinese with their r's, and the Spaniards with their w's. "How did you get here?" he insisted.

"We're from Iloilo, across the strait," I said haltingly, not sure how much to reveal to our captor. "We sailed here on a small boat we built ourselves."

"Ip you American, why aren't you in concentration camp?" he pursued reasonably, peering intently at Lawson.

Feeling it was time for him to intervene in the dialogue, Lawson volunteered: "It's a long story. My folks died during the invasion and his family adopted me. I'm his brother now. But the Japs didn't buy the adoption story. They're now looking for me to send me off to concentration camp. We escaped to your island before they could close in on me."

"We arrived yesterday," I added. "He was wounded by a *jabalina* up there and needs medical attention," I said, pressing our moral advantage with an unsubtle appeal to pity.

Even in the waning light of day, it was apparent that the guerrilla's original bewilderment and bluster were slowly giving way to understanding and compassion. Slipping his weapon's safety latch on, he slung the firearm smartly across his shoulder and approached to give Lawson a hand.

"Pirst, we look at your wound," he said, in a voice clearly accustomed to command.

"Sit here," he ordered Lawson, motioning him to a rock nearby. Pulling a sharp pen knife out of one of his odd, many-pocketed pants, he cut the soiled bandage off Lawson's leg with a deft motion of the wrist. The wound lay bare.

"Not too bad," he commented reassuringly. "Deep, but not bad." He pried open his knapsack, rummaging through it until he found the bundle of small packets he was looking for. Tearing the end off one of them, he poured its white powdery contents on Lawson's wound.

"*Waay na'ng bakukang!*" he proclaimed, slipping into his native tongue as if to pronounce some voodoo magic against the dread tropical infection.

"*Gnaa?*" Why, I asked, puzzled. I knew how long Luis had suffered with his own *bakukang* leg sore. It was still festering, after months of treatment.

"This powder is magic. It's called Sulpa. Made in U.S.A." He paused for a while, as if weighing the need for further explanation. Our questioning looks drew no further information from him. He must have felt a little uncomfortable disclosing military information to two young strangers who could, understandably, blow his operation if caught and tortured. He covered the wound with gauze and wrapped a clean bandage neatly around the leg.

"*Ano'ng gnalan mo?*" asked Lawson expansively, inquiring our friend's name.

"Antonio. I'm Quartermaster op the Central guerrilla group in Jordan, in charge of armament and supplies in this island," he announced with a hint of self importance. We were struck by our luck, stumbling upon such an important personage.

"Are there any Japs in the island?" I asked hesitantly, as we struggled down the mountain. The question had lain in our minds like a bad dream, ever since we landed on the island.

"There used to be a small garrison here, long ago, but no more. They sail prom Iloilo to Jordan in their launches now and then, but only stay long enough por short show-op-porce patrols. Then, they go back, usually the same day," he said. "They don't stray too par inland, either. They're scared of us now," he added self-importantly.

"I bet you could wallop them properly," Lawson commented wryly. I gave him a furtive frown, but the silent warning was unnecessary; the subtle sarcasm had gone unnoticed. Indeed, Antonio had taken the comment as some sort of compliment.

Evening closed slowly, the dark lurking now behind the trees. As the path broke out of a ragged fringe of trees into a clearing, we saw a nipa hut, standing derelict, in the middle of the vaguely familiar upland meadow. It was the same hut we had slept in the night before!

Lawson's leg was sore from the long, downhill hike, and we had to help him up the rickety stairs. Moonlight streamed into the dark room through the open windows. Antonio picked up the bamboo container that hung from the wall and went to fetch some water from the nearby brook. Meanwhile, I started a fire, using kindling I found under the house.

"I'm a great help, aren't I," said Lawson apologetically, as he sat on a corner, resting his throbbing leg. I could tell he was feeling sorry for himself.

"You're just lucky with that Sulfa thing he put on your wound," I answered between puffs, as I tried to get the fire going. "Luis could sure use some of that stuff on his *bakukang*! I'll ask Antonio for a packet or two when we go back to Iloilo."

Antonio returned shortly after. Before long, he had some rice cooking in the blackened pot. That, and some bananas was all we'd have for supper that evening. He promised he'd take us down to have the town doctor work on the wound, first thing in the morning. His wife would feed us properly after that, he added. Things were starting to look up.

Lawson and I shared the worn mat, as we had the previous night. The filtered moonlight streaming into the room through the wide open window made dappled, shifting patterns on the bamboo floor. Snuggled up to his weapon, Antonio was soon snoring in his corner of the room.

"I'm starting to miss home already," whispered Lawson wistfully. "I don't mean just the comforts of home. I mean Mom and Dad and Luis."

I smiled in the dark, touched by the way he felt about the family. He had blended into it so effortlessly, and had become one of us in the brief span of three years. We seldom talked about what would happen after the war, but we both sensed that we'd go our separate ways, he to Scotland and its moors, I to the sweet upland greens of the Pyrenees. But those were far and future things. Meanwhile, there were memories to be made and tucked away. In the earnest struggle for survival, daydreaming and nostalgia somehow seemed like impractical luxuries.

12. THE TIGHTENING NOOSE

The Jordan village clinic was bright with day. Its single room was spartanly furnished with a solitary stainless steel table, a swivel stool and a glass cabinet, replete with neatly lined clamps and scalpels, even some small, chipped, kidney-shaped enamel pans. The overhead lamp that hung limply over the table had probably shed no light since the war broke out.

Lawson lay face down on the examination table. Standing over him on a footstool, was Dr. Manúud. The village doctor was salivating as he pricked the white flesh with a long, curved needle, deftly guiding the suture through the quivering slit of the wound. He tugged determinedly at the string after each stitch until the once gaping wound was sewn into a neat pink slit. To the left and right of it stood little knots, like paired sentinels standing watch over the sutured wound.

"*Ay abaw, ka tahúm!*" murmured the diminutive doctor to himself when he was done with his seamstressing. He tarried a while longer on the footstool, contemplating his handiwork with obvious approval. It was, I agreed, a thing of beauty.

"Not eben Dr. Conally from Mayo Clinic could hab done better," gushed the pixy young nurse, who seemed to be repressing an urge to hug the basking doctor. She found release, instead, cutting her bright black eyes at Lawson, as she dawdled with the dressing.

"It's a shame you folks don't have more casualties around here," said Lawson with deadpan expression. "You'd be a bleeding plastic surgeon in no time flat." I could tell he was feeling no pain, despite the anesthetic-free procedure he'd just undergone.

"Come to tink op it, I neber much cared for Hematology when I was in Med School," admitted the doctor expansively, totally unaware of the Scot's twanging barb. I had to avert Lawson's bemused look to avoid cracking up and spoiling the warmth of the fleeting instant.

"I want to see you in tree days," said the doctor, helping Lawson down from the operating table. The physician stood by the door, a full six inches shorter than his patient. And Lawson was no giant. "We'll take the stitches out then. Meanwhile, try to keep the wound dry."

We thanked him profusely and walked out the front door into the bright December sunlight. Antonio was sitting on the front steps waiting for us, smoking a foul smelling stogie. After helping Lawson get on the mare, he untied the beast from the hitching post and proceeded down the town's main dirt road.

It was hard to pass unnoticed in the crowd. Children stopped in midstride to ogle us. Their bashful curiosity and the yellow dirt road on which they were playing marbles reminded me a little of the Munchkins, in the Wizard of Oz. They tagged along for a while until Antonio finally shooed them away, sending them back to their game.

The faint smell of fish which pervaded the town grew stronger as we approached the marketplace, by the seashore. An old woman was observing our progress from under the palm leaf awning of a flimsy lean-to stall. Spitting out the betel nut cud she was chewing on, she beamed us a red, half toothless grin, in friendly welcome.

"*Magandang arau,*" she greeted in Tagalog, suspecting that we were from out of town and would, therefore, understand the national language better than the local Visayan dialect.

"*Isdâ ko presko gid!*" she bragged, pointing at the fish spread atop her wooden counter, stacked neatly in threes and fours on individual banana leaves. She need not have bothered advertising the freshness of her wares; the mullet and milkfish were still wriggling in their death throes, as if trying to shake off the swarm of pesky flies converging on their slowly glazing eyes.

Antonio pointed at some *bangús* bonefish and ordered a small slab of purplish *guinamús* shrimp paste. The old lady wrapped them expertly in separate banana leaves and handed us the packages. Licking the tip of a small pencil, she wrote down the transaction in a little black notebook that she had extracted from somewhere deep inside her loose blouse. With a reddish grin, she bade us a jovial farewell as we departed.

Jose Maria Lacambra

On the way home, Antonio led us through back roads to keep the attraction to a minimum. Sunlight laid across the thatched nipa roofs and gathered in silent pools along the potholed alleys. We ambled alongside the mare on which Lawson rode, slowly wending our way towards the outskirts of town, near the foothills.

"You will stay with us por the time being," said Antonio. "There's plenty op room and plenty op pood. War will soon be ober and you can go back to your own home. Meanwhile, you are welcome in mine."

"Thanks," I said, touched by his generosity, "but you've already done enough for us. We'd hate to get you in trouble if the Japs come along looking for us."

"Nonsense!" he blurted out, offended by the hint of rejected hospitality. "You will be saper in my place than anywhere else. I know where to hide you ip there's trouble. So no more talk about it," he added huffily.

We trudged along in silence, raising small puffs of dust with every step. Despite the lateness of the year, the sun stared down at us with the anger of noon, pouring down shimmering barbs of golden heat. As we walked along the row of nipa huts, window curtains twitched imperceptively, concealing the curious stares of natives who had seldom seen foreign visitors from the mainland, let alone the younger variety.

The flimsy, single room houses were built almost entirely of bamboo, from the supporting stilts and rickety ladder to the floors and woven mats that served as walls, all gracefully topped by a thatch of palm leaves. The distinctive architecture

138

had remained unchanged over centuries of ancestral Malayan design. Easy to build, the pliant structures were designed to survive the sway of earthquakes and be quickly rebuilt if flattened by the typhoons which frequently savaged these islands.

We finally arrived at Antonio's home. The two-story structure at the edge of town reminded me a little of the one we had rented in Igbarás, when we fled from the Japanese, several years earlier. It stood apart from the rest of the habitations, surrounded by lush fields of truck farming. A riot of bougainvillea blossoms lent a touch of color to the dwelling.

Climbing the wooden steps to the landing, we were ushered into a pleasant, sun-bright parlor. A lithograph of the Sacred Heart of Jesus gazed down benignly from behind the cracked glass, held together by a wooden frame.

Three naked tots, ranging in age from one to four, were playing fiddlesticks on the rag carpet in the middle of the living room. The two older boys jumped up the moment they saw their father walk in, and ran over to greet him boisterously. Not about to miss any of the excitement, the baby girl wobbled to her feet and waddled over to us. They all hung on to Antonio during the introductions, peeking at us from around and under their father's legs with soulful, saucer-sized black eyes.

A plump, pleasant looking woman in her early thirties, walked in from the kitchen, moments later. Antonio's wife was carrying a baby astride her hip, held by a large bandana wrapped around her shoulder.

"Malíng, these are the two boys I talked to you about this morning after dropping them opp at the doctor's. They'll be staying with us por a while."

"Hello," she said cheerily, flashing us a warm smile. "Welcome to our home. Did the doctor hurt you much?" she asked Lawson with motherly concern.

"Not really," answered Lawson, pleased with the attention.

"I'm glad. It'll heal sooner than you think." I noticed her easy command of the English language. It was unusually good, for country folk. "You poor boys must be starved," she said. "Come, dinner is ready."

She laid the baby in a crib while Antonio ushered us into the small dining room. From her wall-mounted pedestal, a statue of the Immaculate Conception dominated the room. We all sat around the circular table, amidst the din of excited children. The finely embroidered pineapple cloth placemats under the china suggested something other than a humdrum meal. The occasion must have called not only for finery but, I half hoped, the leftovers of some fatted sow.

Malíng was as good a short-order cook as she was a gracious hostess. They may have been leftovers but the mere sight of the small dishes she started serving brought on small twinges of urgent salivation. First came the *lumpiâ* egg rolls and *pansít* vegetables, followed by the pungent adobo chicken and *sugp*ó shrimp, all native delicacies which I remembered drooling over in our help's dining room before the war. After the prescribed blessing, we all dug into the bowls, and made short shrift of the exotic meal.

A lively after-dinner conversation followed. Having taught English in the local school, Malíng was intrigued by Lawson's brogue and quaint turn of phrase. She was mortified when corrected for referring to him as English, but laughed graciously and proceeded to other subjects. Innately curious, she eventually extracted details of our background and adventures which her husband would never have bothered asking.

"You were lucky to have stumbled on my Antonio," she said looking at her husband with undisguised pride and affection. "He holds an important position in the local guerrilla organization and may be able to help you in more ways than you think," she said, reaching over to squeeze his hand in an affectionate gesture.

"Meanwhile," she added, "as I'm sure Antonio has told you, our home is your home. You are welcome here por as long as you remain in Guimarás. We have plenty op room, and the farm is bountipul."

"Thanks," I said inadequately, touched by the warm and simple grace with which she offered us her home. "We'll try to help around the house to earn our keep," I volunteered.

"Yeah, we worked on Victory plots back home," Lawson added. "Probably we can help with the farm work, or something."

Antonio took us up on our offer. We were knee deep in farm chores before long. Lawson's leg had healed nicely, after a few weeks. The two of us tried to make ourselves useful around the farm, mending fences and feeding chickens and threshing rice. Some days we'd baby-sit while Malíng went to town, shopping or visiting friends. The days went by unnoticed, life so full and peaceable that nostalgia waned, first a little and then altogether forgotten.

In Jordan, we discovered a green new world full of pulsing scents and exotic flowers. We learned, firsthand, about things that grew and multiplied, and sometimes stung and kicked. Nature's strange ways of preserving the species intrigued us. In juvenile wonder, we gawked at the magnificent ritual of mating horses, and were amused by roosters, strutting about their stamping grounds amidst arguing chickens, and the little corkscrew organs male pigs brandished tirelessly, in their endless mating.

Pakíng, the young acolyte of the local mission church, befriended us.

"Wanna ride my racehorse?" he asked one day. Its owner had shipped the thoroughbred out to Guimarás when the war broke out, for safekeeping, entrusting it to Pakíng's care.

"You gotta be carepul with it," he said, helping me up on the restless horse. "I made the reins myselp out op rubber tire strips. They stretch too much," he admitted. "And another thing," he added, "It only knows one speed, and that's plat out."

You could tell, just by looking at it, that impatience coursed through the thoroughbred's veins. It was always snorting, as if displeased with all this grazing and enforced inactivity. I ribbed the horse gingerly at first, to get a feel for the way it handled. The magnificent beast leapt forward with eager stride, covering ground with thunderous speed. Riding it was like riding the wind, and just about as hard to tame.

A short while later, I noticed that the horse was totally ignoring my tug at the makeshift reins. The reason suddenly dawned on me; Antonio's mare, which Lawson was riding nearby, was in heat. Catching her scent, the rutting stallion took off after her, at full tilt. Gasping for breath, I hung on to the useless reins as the horse's mane slapped my wind-drawn face.

"Jump off!" I shouted at Lawson, as the distance between us closed. But he, too, was galloping hard and could barely hear me. We flew through town, chickens scampering and natives gawking.

Lawson eventually caught on to his predicament and managed to steer his mare into some farmer's barn, shutting the door behind him, just in time. My stallion finally came to a disconsolate halt.

Evenings, Lawson and I would ride Antonio's mare to the beach for a swim. Seeming to sense the end of light, the sea water shimmered with its own strange phosphorescence, robing our nakedness with a thousand lingering sequins of light, long after we'd surfaced from the water.

One afternoon, several weeks after we'd moved in with them, Antonio asked Lawson and me to come with him to an important meeting that was to be held in town, later that evening. There was almost an air of conspiracy in his request.

"What's it about?" I asked, intrigued by the odd request.

"It's our weekly war planning meeting. There's talk op suspicious Japanese launch actibity in Iloilo. Probably

143

preparing por a raid on our island. We must decide where to hide you, just in case."

"Well, that should stir up a wee bit of excitement around here," said Lawson, trying to relieve the tension he sensed in Antonio's voice with a touch of levity.

Darkness had fallen by the time we gathered under the canopy of a huge banyan tree in the outskirts of town. The choice of meeting ground surprised me; either these islanders were unaware of the tree's *pasmo* curse or something else, like the phase of the moon or the number of *iguana* lizard "to-ko" croaks, was voiding the curse. About a dozen men were gathered round a camp fire, its flickering light casting eerie shadows behind the huddled group. Someone was raising a telescopic antenna from what looked like a transmitter-receiver set.

Antonio exchanged passwords with the group's sentry, who saluted smartly before allowing us into the assembly. Lawson and I exchanged glances, impressed by the ritual. After the proper introductions, we all sat around the feeble fire and made small talk.

The meeting was eventually called to order by a tall, lean man. His granny glasses gave him a certain professorial air, while his jungle camouflage garb and shiny lapel emblems were unmistakable symbols of command. The group's secretary, a short man with a 'keedle' look about him, droned on about past action items, about which nobody seemed to show any overwhelming interest.

The tall bespectacled man positioned himself in the center of the group to address the gathering. Except for the occasional rustle of banyan leaves in the night breeze, there was dead silence when he finally spoke.

"I'd like to extend a warm welcome to our priends from Iloilo," he said in a deep, carrying voice, looking in our direction. "Despite their young age," he continued, "I hear that they hab already done more por the cause than some of us hab, or perhaps, eber will. They are guerrillas in the best tradition and are to be commended."

Murmurs of approval and a round of ragged applause followed.

"But I'm apraid the enemy may be apter them," he continued. "Intelligence sources indicate the Kempitai hab been visiting these boys' home during the past seberal days. No one has been arrested, that we know op, but they could hab twisted someone's arm or there could hab been a leak."

He paused for effect, before continuing. "At any rate, there's been an unusual amount op actibity in the Iloilo wharp yesterday and today. There's been much coming and going and loading op ammunition and troop gear onto several launches. A raid seems to be in the opping. Now, it could merely be an end-run tactic to break their siege. But then again, it could be a raid on Guimarás."

"The blighters!" said Lawson under his breath, surprised and disturbed by the disquieting turn of events.

I, too, was stunned by the news, not so much by the prospects of being hunted down as by the fear that harm might have befallen someone back home. Dad could be arrested and tortured. After all, hadn't they jailed Mr. Xaudaró for the much more trivial offense of keeping a short-wave radio? A flurry of waking nightmares flitted across my consciousness in rapid succession, leaving behind a gnawing sense of remorse. Lawson, who was sitting next to me, reached over and grabbed my arm.

"I'm terribly sorry about all the bother I've brought on them," he whispered, his voice breaking slightly. "I shouldn't have put them through all this trouble. It was really selfish of me."

I noticed his eyes glistening in the campfire's feeble light.

"It's gonna be O.K.," I reassured him, gripping the hand resting on my arm. "They don't have a shred of evidence until they catch us. And we won't let them do that, will we?"

Antonio's voice cut through our self pity during a lull in our private exchange. He had been talking to the group for a while but we only caught the tail end of his address.

"...and I think the Navy should conduct the rescue operation," he was saying with emphasis. "Apter all, they've done it bepore in Panay. Remember that pamily they had on board the sub during their last supply call here? They were taking them to Australia. And they weren't even prom a belligerent country. They were only Swiss, for Chrissakes!"

"But we're not due por another supply drop until next month," said the tall commander equably, "and our problem does have a certain urgency about it. This raid is imminent, like tomorrow, perhaps. Certainly no later than the day apter. Why, they might be sailing tonight, eben!"

146

The radio, sitting on a wooden box propped up against the trunk of the enormous banyan tree, suddenly came to life, emitting squawking noises amidst the simple hiss of distance. Everyone fell silent as they turned to watch the operator, who fiddled nervously with the dials.

"This is SN-X calling Hummer-2. Come in, Hummer-2," croaked a distinctively nasal American voice through the garbled roar and sibilant twits of static.

The voice gave me goose bumps. I could almost picture a sub commander, the spitting image of Cary Grant, talking in a cramped radio room, sporting a small Lt. Commander's star on the neck of his wilted, sweat-stained Khaki shirt, puffing on a Camel cigarette. The drama of the image overwhelmed me.

The lanky troop commander approached the radio and picked up the speaker phone handed him by Sparky.

"This is Hummer-2, come in SN-X."

"We're in the neighborhood. Could make a drop if coast is clear. What's the situation? Over."

"Negatib. We're expecting unpriendlies any time. Try again next scheduled call. By the way, you may be picking up a couple of passengers on your next stop. Ober."

"Roger. Over and out."

The radio operator turned the transmitter off, surprising the night life in a rare moment of rapt attention, wary of the strange radio hisses and gurgles. The nocturnal clamor crept back cautiously, one sound at a time, like reluctant instruments in a practicing orchestra. First came the tentative croak of frogs, followed by little shivers of cricket song and a distant cock's crow. The lovesick call of an iguana brought the dubious symphony to its original clamor. The sweet scent of sampaguita flowers wafting across the night air, lent unity and meaning to the tropical cacophony.

"Sorry, young pellows," said the bespectacled commander, looking balefully at Lawson and me. "You could have been on your way to Australia. But there'll be time por that later on. Meanwhile we must get you opp to some sape place." Looking at Antonio, he asked: "Any suggestions?"

Arms across his chest, Antonio had been standing, deep in thought, fingers of a free hand pulling pensively at his lower lip.

"I've been tinking," he said, snapping out of his reverie. "Perhaps the cave behind the waterpall might not be a bad hiding place por them. It's near enough the depot cave so we can supply them easily with rations."

"Good tinking!" said the commander of the troop after mulling over Antonio's suggestion. "It's settled then. You can take them up there yourself tomorrow, at pirst light. Give them each a carbine and show them how to use them. They made need them. They're old enough to handle firearms." Signaling it was time for Antonio to take Lawson and me back to his home, he added snappily: "You're excused."

The meeting continued on into the night. With the likelihood of an imminent raid on the island, there were tactics to be ironed out and assignments to be made.

13. TARGET PRACTICE

A brittle December rain was falling when we left the house early the next morning. Malíng stood by the door, a worried look in her eyes despite the brave smile she managed to beam at us, as she waved us off.

"Be carepul, my children. I want you back sape and sound."

Antonio led the way, trudging along in hunched silence, following the rocky trail toward the beckoning heights. Like Malíng, he, too, brooded on dark omens which he kept to himself. The mare would have provided easy uphill transportation for at least two of us, but it had needed shoeing and there had been no time for that.

"You wouldn't happen to remember the name of that family the Commander spoke of last night, would you?" I asked, more to break the oppressive silence than to satisfy any consuming curiosity. "You know, the Swiss passengers on the sub," I clarified.

"Not really," Antonio answered, breathing heavily now. "It was one of those long poreign names. They were a middle-aged couple, with tree or pour children about your age. They looked haggard, like they'd been through the wringer up there in the Panay hills. Constantly on the move, evading Japs, they said."

"Their name wouldn't happen to have been Guemperle, by any chance, would it?" I asked, intrigued now.

"Yes!" he said, suddenly recognizing the name. "They were taking some presh air on the deck while we unloaded supplies. I got to talk a bit with the young boy. Nice pellow. Did you know them, then?"

"Sure did! They're good friends of the family. The boy's name is Fritz. He and I used to go bird hunting around Igbarás, near Igtalongón. Did you say they were headed for Australia?"

"Yes, that's where they usually take them," he answered.

"Must be a nice place, Australia," Lawson chimed in. "Boy, wouldn't it be neat if we got to go there! I wonder where we'd stay, though."

"The British Embassy would take care of you, I'm sure," I volunteered. "I don't really think I want to go that far away from home, especially with things the way they are right now," I added pensively. The thought of Uyeki's snooping around the house looking for us had been nagging at me. I knew that Lawson's adoption papers were on the up and up, but wondered about their timing. Lawson and I had discussed that fine point before, and agreed it was a bit shaky.

Trying to steer my thoughts away from the gnawing worry about home, I asked Antonio: "When do you suppose the Yanks will land in Panay?" suspecting, even as I asked, that he'd have no deeper insight into the Americans' landing plans than I did.

"Hard to tell. They're still mopping up in Leyte. And that might just be a jumping opp point to somewhere up north. Apter all, island hopping is MacArthur's trade mark. He's been at it por the past couple op years now. He may bypass the rest op the islands altogether, on his way to Tokyo. That's his pinal goal, you know. We'll just hab to wait and see."

"It doesn't seem fair, grand-standing his return to some obscure island, just so he can say he kept his promise," I answered, with ill-concealed indignation.

"Local history is going to judge him harshly ip he pulled that one on the Pilipinos," agreed Antonio without wholly discarding the possibility. "What's worse," he added, "is that the isolated Japanese army could make things miserable for the civilian population lept behind, like so many stranded hostages."

I mulled over the unpromising prospects in silence, as we continued trekking uphill. Things were starting to look pretty bleak, all of a sudden.

It had stopped drizzling by the time we reached the denser canopy of the forest. The air there was dark, blanketing the trail in dim and strange ways. Occasional shafts of sunlight pierced the gloom, speckling the leaf-strewn path underfoot. The wildlife's clamor bounced around the thickets, pausing only in the little pocket of jungle immediately surrounding us. We stopped for a drink at a brook crossing, and proceeded uphill, panting, deep in somber thought. There was little joy in the climb that morning.

We gained the heights several hours later. Directly ahead of us stood the impossible verticality of a cliff rising high above the crowns of enormous eucalyptus trees. Carefully, we followed a narrow ledge that wound precariously along the granite face of the sheer mountain side. Abruptly, the trail disappeared into a dark opening yawning vacantly, in the face of the mountain.

Antonio disappeared in the cave while Lawson and I stood near the entrance, letting our eyes get used to the darkness inside. Somewhere in the bowels of the cave, Antonio struck a match and lit a kerosene lamp. He was now walking slowly toward the entrance, to illumine our way.

"You can come in now," he said, his voice bouncing around the cave walls in receding echoes. The lamp's flame threw its flickering redness all around, casting eerie shadows on the loaf-like rocks that studded the walls of the large enclosure. The dirt floor slanted slightly downward toward the cave's opening, where several large rocks jutted out from the ground.

The dank air inside had a primeval smell about it. The musty scent conjured up scenes from cherished Rice Burroughs science fiction stories.

"Smells like one of those caves in 'Man from Mars' doesn't it," I commented.

"Is that the one about the space travelers who survive on pockets of stale oxygen left behind by an extinct civilization?" asked Lawson.

"That's the one!"

We sat on the smooth rocky outcroppings near the entrance of the cave, and opened the care package that Malíng had hurriedly prepared for us, the night before. The climb had made us hungry, and we made short shrift of the left-over *lumpiâ* and *poto* rice buns she had wrapped in a banana leaf.

"Time to go to work," said Antonio, when we finished lunch. Prying open one of the wooden boxes stacked up against the interior wall of the cave, he pulled out two large plastic bags from it, each containing a generously greased carbine rifle. We spent the better part of an hour wiping the green goop from the short, lightweight weapons.

As I wiped the remaining grease from my firearm, it began to dawn on me that these guerrillas must have considered our situation pretty desperate to furnish weapons to a couple of teenagers. Sobered by the disquieting thought, I prodded Antonio:

"Do you really think we'll be needing these?"

"I sincerely hope not," he responded, "but one neber knows. I will teach you how to work these weapons. You must respect them and exercise great care and good judgment ip and when you hab to use them. But you must always remember the guerrilla code: 'Stealth is health'. Neber reveal your position unless you hab a clear abenue op escape. You are here to hide, not to pight. These weapons should be used only as a last resort."

The cheery pep talk left me wondering more than ever why we were being provided weapons they'd rather we wouldn't use. Lawson looked just as perplexed by the contradiction, but managed to turn the dark advice into one of his lighthearted quips:

"I like that 'stealth is health' bit. How about 'Give 'em hell without a bell'?" He smiled at his own witticism. "We're pretty good at that. You needn't worry about us."

Antonio smiled at the Scot's quick grasp of guerrilla tactical doctrine. "My Commander showed good judgment letting you two join our troop," he remarked. "But remember," he added soberly, "we don't hand out many medals in our outpit."

Stuffing several ammunition clips into his knapsack, Antonio led the way out of the cave. We followed the ledge and struck off toward the craggy heights. Gaining the ridge an hour later, we started target practice after a few elementary lessons in weapon handling.

We started shooting at an empty can from about a hundred paces. The firearm's almost negligible recoil felt like a gentle shove on the shoulder. The carbine seemed ideally suited for jungle warfare, where one had little time to aim, just shoot from the hip, in one fast reflex action. The semiautomatic's short barrel may have been great for close combat but did little for marksmanship at long range.

"Bob Steele used to shoot from the hip in the movies," I commented. "Even while galloping on his horse. He was good at it, too!" I tried shooting the firearm in that guise, and managed to hit the can after only three attempts.

"Good show!" commented Lawson. He was about to copy me when Antonio spoke up.

"You're wasting precious ammunition," he said, frowning.

So we went back to shoulder aiming until we eventually ran out of ammunition. It was mid afternoon by the time we returned to the cave. We spent the rest of the afternoon learning how to take the weapon apart, clean it and put it together again. Lawson didn't need any instruction in that department.

"Let me try to figure it out myself," he begged Antonio.

Before even waiting for an answer, he had started disassembling the semiautomatic's intricate mechanism. Absorbed in exquisite concentration, Lawson started humming to himself, tongue flicking in and out of his lips, while emitting pleasurable grunts. He had the pieces strewn all over the *petate* mat in no time, fondling the springs and bolts as if they were animate objects. He cleaned the pieces and had them all back together in place long before I'd even finished disassembling my weapon.

"You're all thumbs, aren't you," he mocked, watching me struggle with my firearm's springs and bolts.

"Yeah, they make great knuckle sandwiches!" I replied, shaking a greasy fist at him.

Antonio listened to the lighthearted banter with bemused smile. He seemed pleased with our day's progress.

Darkness had fallen by the time I finished cleaning my weapon. It was then I realized we hadn't shot a thing for supper.

"We'd better go hunt for some food," I proposed.

Antonio ignored the suggestion. He shuffled, instead, to a pile of charred stones near the entrance of the cave, where he started a small fire, using some kindling stacked near the cave entrance. From a satchel that hung from the wall, he extracted a mess kit and an olive-green, wax-covered carton, the size of a cigar box. By the flickering firelight, I read the mysterious word 'K-Rations' written on it.

After balancing the mess kit's platter over the tentative fire, he slit open the carton with his pocket knife. From it, he extracted several small tin cans and small packets, laying the trove on the *petate* mat he had dragged over by the fire.

Lawson and I looked on with mounting curiosity. Our mouths began to water in anticipation, sensing some exotic meal in the offing. Tearing open one of the small, olive-colored packets, Antonio emptied its yellowish contents into the mess kit's drinking cup. After pouring water on the powder, he stirred the concoction with a spoon and poured the broth into the heating pan. Prying open a can containing several tiny sausages, he laid them alongside the now sizzling scrambled eggs. The smell of eggs and sausage permeated the cave, raising pangs of hunger to a gnawing pitch.

Antonio passed the frying pan around when the food was done. Using our fingers, we each took turns picking bite-sized morsels from it. Antonio watched with bemused smile as we munched on the delicious meal, emitting occasional grunts of pleasure with tummy-patting gestures of sheer content.

"How about a little dessert?" asked Antonio after we'd wolfed down the main course. Using his knife, he sliced a small chocolate bar into three equal portions, giving us each a piece. Unwrapping the cover, we popped the hard brown portion into our mouths, where it slowly melted. I closed my eyes for a second and was a child again, knowing exactly why Hershey had labeled those little chocolate drops of theirs 'Kisses'. I suddenly realized how aptly they'd been named.

The surprises spilling from the unpretentious little K-Rations carton never seemed to cease. The powdery contents of another packet were quickly transformed into a canteen full of orange juice, which we gulped down greedily. Finally, Lawson and I shared a stick of Wrigley's Spearmint chewing gum, while Antonio pocketed a small pack containing three Chesterfield cigarettes. The last remaining item in the amazing cornucopia brought on a chuckle; neatly folded in a slender packet were half a dozen olive-colored squares of toilet paper.

"Do Yanks eat like this in the battlefield all the time?" I asked Antonio incredulously, remembering the frugal bowl of rice and the measly sardine which seemed to suffice the Japanese soldiers.

"Even better!" said Antonio, lighting up one of his Chesterfields. "In the Navy, anyway. Believe it or not, soldiers actually hate K-Rations," he added cryptically. The thought defied belief.

Lying back on the *petate* mat near the entrance of the cave, Antonio watched the swirls of cigarette smoke rising lazily out of the cave and into the moonlit night outside.

"Well," he said when he had finished smoking, "Guess it's time to hit the sack. It's been a long day and we gotta get up early tomorrow to move on to the other cave."

"What other cave?" I asked.

"The one you'll hide in. It's not sape to remain in this one. It's hard to obserb anyone approaching along the ledge. Besides, we don't want to compromise this weapons depot. The other cave is nearby and is even harder to pind. You'll see."

Despite only a tarpaulin for a mattress, sleep was not long coming that night. Somewhere in the jungle outside, an iguana shattered the silence with its raucous 'to-ko', and then it was quiet again, except for the crickets and a pining frog in the distance. Splintered moonlight slithered up the cave's entrance, holding out its silver offering. Strange, how little it takes for youth to regain faith in life's goodness; only a full stomach suffices, sometimes.

Jose Maria Lacambra

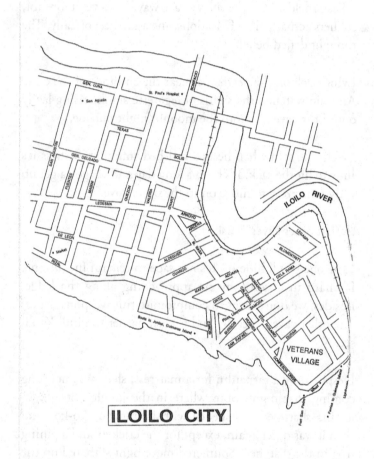

ILOILO CITY

160

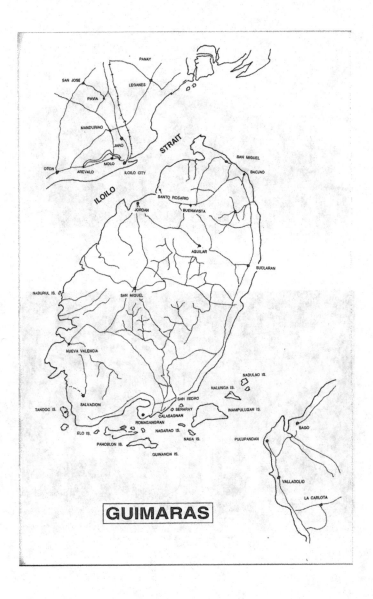

Front view of Author's home in Iloilo

Second Grade class picture (1938), Colegio San Agustin, Iloilo.
Author, then aged 7, is in second row, far right.

Author's parents, in Baguio.

The cave in Guimarás, visited by Author, 50 years later.

Original message dropped by artillery spotter, prompting bombardment halt.(Museo de Iloilo archives).

Lt. Jac Chambliss (one of first American Officers who
liberated the Lacambras on March 1945) later to become
author's father-in-law

Author (right) with brother, Luis, at war's end.

Author, aged 16, on return trip to Spain after war.

14. THE CAVE

We moved out of the cave shortly after dawn, the next morning. Gingerly, we edged our way along the narrow ledge, each weighed down with a carbine and a knapsack, filled with a few clips of ammunition and some K-rations.

"I feel like there's something missing," said Lawson, trying not to look down at the abyss. "Fifes and drums, that's it! Perhaps a few whiffs of cordite to add character to it all."

"We may be smelling that sooner than you think," I said soberly. "I wonder what we're doing, loaded down like battle-scarred warriors."

"Makes you feel kind'a grown up before your time, don't it," he said.

"Yeah, they say one ages quickly in the eve of battle, but this is ridiculous!"

The footpath meandered some distance into the forest, slipping in and out of sunlight. Abandoning the trail after a while, we slid down a steep slope, taking a shortcut to the little brook we had crossed the day before. Following the stream uphill for a short distance, we came upon a small, secluded pool near a sunlit glen.

It was a place of strange enchantment. A small waterfall crashed into the shallow pool with splashing scandal. Feeding on the gossamer mists, patches of velvet lichen and moss paused at the edge of the pool, as if to observe their own image in the water's shimmering mirror, blurred by reflections of trees stood on their heads.

As we approached the far edge of the pool, a pair of cockatoos flew off into the warm air, squawking their displeasure.

"Watch out," warned Antonio. "The rocks are very slippery."

Treading carefully over them, we followed Antonio as he wove his way around the pool. We wedged ourselves between the cascade and the sweaty granite of the mountain wall and then, quite unexpectedly, found ourselves inside the cave.

"Wow!" said Lawson in hushed tones. "What a place!" The roar of the cascade outside had become subdued, replaced by a quiet coziness in the cave's interior. Light filtering through the waterfall bathed the small enclosure with a strange and tenuous light, dancing as if possessed with a life of its own.

"The other cave, the arms depot one, had a blind approach," said Antonio. "This one has an unobstructed view op anyone approaching. A little blurred by the waterpall, perhaps, but a clear shot. There should be no surprises ip you are vigilant."

Antonio sat down and lit a cigarette. I noticed how the smoke drifted out toward the entrance, suggesting another opening, somewhere in the bowels of the cave, from where the draft originated.

Antonio showed us where the essentials were stored in the cave, pointing at a kerosene lamp hanging from a wall, the inevitable petate roll propped up under it, and the firewood piled up near the entrance.

"The temperature in these caves is always the same; a perfect twenty two degrees Centigrade. And, oh by the way, there's bats in this cave."

Lawson and I looked at each other apprehensively.

"Don't worry. They're actually quite priendly. They keep the cave pree of mosquitoes."

After he finished his cigarette, Antonio got up and looked around. He appeared restive.

"Well, I'll have to go now," he said. "Got to get back to my pamily. It's a long hike back and, por all I know, the Japanese may be back in Guimarás." He shuffled over to the cave entrance, making as if to leave. It was almost noon.

"I believe you hab everything you need por now. Don't eat all the K-Rations the pirst day. They've gotta last a while. I'll come and check up on you, now and then. And another thing; Don't wander too par prom the cave. And, whatever you do, don't make too much noise, or all this hiding will be por naught. Take care op yourselves!" he said, shaking our hands in formal farewell. "Good luck! I'll see you soon."

He slipped out of the cave and disappeared into the forest, behind a blur of water.

"What a guy!" said Lawson. "That's what I call a friend!"

"He's sure gone to a lot of trouble to get us out here when he's got his own family to worry about," I added.

"Isn't this some kind'a hideout, though!" commented Lawson, still awed by the surroundings. "Wonder how anybody ever found this cave, in the first place."

"These folks are pretty forest-smart", I said. "They make great trackers, I've always heard. Keen nose and sharp ears. And stealthy, too. I guess walking around on bare feet helps cut down on the noise."

"I'd sure hate to be surrounded by several thousands of them, like those Japs back in Iloilo," remarked Lawson.

"Those Nips are no slouches, either. That Regiment of troops in Panay didn't survive this long on just good will and Sake toasts. Those long bayonets and god-awful shrieks of theirs can sure put the fear of the Lord in a few guerrillas, don't you think?"

"I wonder if they're really looking for us," said Lawson, changing the subject. "I mean, what's the point? Even if they come and sniff us out, they don't even have a proper ship to take me to that ruddy concentration camp in Manila."

"They probably have something else in mind," I said, thinking about other more dismal options. "Whatever they're up to, we'd better keep one step ahead of them. I don't trust that Uyeki farther than I can throw him." A shiver accompanied the thought.

"Do you know something?" I added. "I don't think hiding out in this cave is such a hot idea, after all."

Lawson looked at me quizzically. "Why?" he asked apprehensively. "What do you mean?"

"Well, there's no way out of this place if they ever came charging up that entrance. We'd be trapped in here like rats."

"That's a cheerful thought! So, what do you suggest we do?"

"Well, for starters, let's look for some other entrance," I proposed. "I noticed earlier some kind of a breeze blowing in here occasionally. Let's check out the cave."

Picking up the kerosene lamp, I lit it, purposely leaving a crack under the glass cover to let the fluttering flame lead us to the source of the breeze. The dank, prehistoric smell grew stronger as we got deeper into the cave. Huge boulders littered the damp, uneven floor. Drops of water met each other slithering down the cave wall, forming small rivulets that meandered into and disappeared in nooks and crannies. Suddenly, we heard a high-pitched squeak coming from somewhere above us.

"This place gives me the creeps," said Lawson apprehensively.

"I think it's pretty spooky, myself." The squeak had caused the hairs on the back of my neck to stand up at attention.

There was a large boulder almost totally obstructing the narrowing passage. Just as I was inching my way around it, the lamp's flame started to dance violently on its wick. It flickered for an instant and then was snuffed out completely by a sudden gust of fresh air. Thrown into complete darkness, our dilated pupils groped for light.

"If you did that on purpose, it's not funny," said Lawson, not amused. "We don't have that many matches left, you know."

"I didn't do it! Honest!" I answered. "There must be an opening above us, somewhere. Don't you feel the breeze?" A faint light shied in and out of peripheral vision as our eyes slowly adapted to the darkness. "I think I see light up there, right above this big rock here. See it?"

"Yeah, I see it!" cried Lawson. "Light that lamp again. See if we can reach the opening. I bet this rock right here left that opening in the roof when it caved in, whenever that was."

"I think you're right!" I said, fumbling for my matches. "We can probably reach the opening if we just climb up on this boulder."

Leaving the lighted lamp on the cave floor, I heaved Lawson up onto the large boulder. As he stood atop it and started groping around the source of light, a sudden clamor of high pitched squeaks emanated from the cave's ceiling, somewhere above him.

"Oh, sod it!" he cried in disgust. "There's a nest of ruddy bats flapping around my face, like they're getting ready to fly up my nose!"

"Just make sure your mouth's shut," I suggested, trying not to laugh at his predicament. "Do you see the opening?" I asked, hoping to get him back on track.

"Yup. There's some sort of root system around the opening where the light's trying to punch through. It's too small to pull ourselves out through it, though."

"You can probably dig some of the dirt out of the way to enlarge the hole," I suggested. "Hope that tree above doesn't come down on us."

"Stand clear of the dirt," he said, starting to claw at the hole above him. Prematurely aroused, the disturbed bat colony started flying past him in a blur of leathery wings, on their confused way out to the cave's main entrance. Minutes later, a large clod of dislodged earth came crashing down from the cave roof, barely missing me. A shaft of blinding sunlight streamed down to the cave floor. Surprised by the sudden brightness, several small, whitish lizards slithered off into the dark safety of the cave's cracks and fissures.

After several frustrated attempts, Lawson finally helped me up the slippery rock on which he was standing. Grabbing on to a large root directly above us, and helped by a little shove from behind, he managed to pull himself up through the opening he'd just widened. When my turn came, I grabbed the root above me with one hand and Lawson's extended hand with the other, and pulled myself up through the opening, into the bright sunlight outside.

We were standing in a patch of ferns surrounding the base of a large Lauan tree that rose majestically above the canopy of the forest. Its roots were moistened by the waters of a small but clamorous stream that disappeared from sight less than a hundred yards farther down the steep slope, rushing headlong into space to crash into the pool below. A monkey eyed us warily from an overhanging branch, emitting occasional squeals as it twitched its tail in uncertain territorial defiance.

"How about that!" cried Lawson, delighted at our feat. "Let's check out the view from the edge," he proposed, tingling with excitement.

Carefully, we inched our way to the precipice and looked down on the panorama below. The falls' roar drowned out all other sounds, its mists curling up lazily above the vault of the forest. Caressed by the sunlight, a small rainbow shimmered above the pool, bathing the scene with an unreal light.

"Let's go for a swim!" I proposed.

"Last one in's a green snot!" rejoined Lawson.

The mad scramble down the steep, slippery slope alongside the waterfall was pierced by howls of pain and laughter. Head over heels, we tumbled into the beckoning pool. We splashed and wrestled in the cool shallow waters, daring each other to stand directly under the falls. Nobody won; it was too painful.

"Let's explore the mountain," I suggested, after we'd dried out in the sun.

"Remember what Antonio said," reminded Lawson.

"Don't worry. It won't take long."

Picking up our carbines, we struck up the steep slope, in a northwesterly direction. Shards of sunlight stole through erratic openings in the matted ceiling of the forest. We followed a footpath which meandered through slanting meadows, tall with saw grass and nettles.

The path came to an abrupt end in a field of jagged rock. A little farther on we reached the familiar broken cliffs. We sat on the rock outcroppings at the edge of the cliff. Faces brushed by the sunny wind, our eyes feasted on the blue sky and green ocean that blended along the distant slit of the horizon. Like a symphony of rough rock and limpid water, the scene captured the eye and absorbed the mind in a tranquil, hypnotic spell.

A brown eagle appeared from nowhere, soaring effortlessly in the sky above us. We watched it glide majestically on the brawny shoulders of the wind, the almost imperceptive twitching of its tail feathers controlling its path in the serene sky. It eyed us with curiosity at first and then ignored us, looking for easier prey. Lowering its head and pulling its wings back against its sleek body, it suddenly screamed downwind in a steep power stoop, disappearing behind the rocky promontory below us.

"It's like a messenger of the gods," remarked Lawson, moved by the majesty and grace of the powerful bird.

"Or an omen?" I said distractedly. I had become aware of the unmistakable drone of a solitary aircraft, somewhere to the east of us. It was definitely American, I knew without the seeing.

"Must be the Lone Ranger," commented Lawson casually.

For several months now, a single-engine Lockheed De Havilland reconnaissance aircraft had come visiting, flying slow circles in the evening sky above town, as if to reassure itself that the island was still there. We had named it after one of our favorite serial movie heroes.

It soon came into view, heading towards Iloilo. Flying a lazy pattern over the city, it was probably counting the ships in the harbor for next day's ritual bombing. As the airplane hummed overhead, on its way back to the vacant skies over Negros, we jumped up and down near the edge of the cliff, waving at it frantically, like kids do at the engineer of a passing train. There was no response.

"Unsociable bugger!" muttered Lawson, smiling. He sniggered every time he uttered something he thought naughty. Many times, that was the only way I could tell some of his funny British expressions were not for polite company. He himself no longer remembered what half of them meant.

We sat for a long time, arms wrapped around our knees, looking dreamily down on Iloilo, wrapped in solitary, peaceful thought, saying nothing. Somewhere, down there, our family was eating the usual supper of Mongo beans with rice, perhaps a little salted pork, followed by a banana for dessert. The thought made me hungry.

A harsh wind started whistling against the rocks as the sun, obese with the distortion of dusk, started dipping into the horizon. It was time to go back to the safety of the cave before it got too dark. As we stood up, a movement at the mouth of the Iloilo River caught our attention.

"I wonder if that's what we've been expecting," I said, pointing at three launches nosing their way out of the Iloilo River, into open waters.

"Strange time of day to be going anywhere on a friendly visit," reflected Lawson, suspicious of the late maritime activity. "Probably just night fishing for sardines or something."

"Let's wait and see where they're headed," I suggested.

Sailing in close formation, the three launches cut a single V-shaped ripple in the becalmed waters. Shortly after, the watery arrowhead was pointing ominously at Guimarás, maintaining an unerring course toward Jordan. It was a landing party; there was little doubt about it now.

"Well, that settles that," I said. "We'd better hustle on back to the cave and lie low for a while."

"Persistent little bleeder, isn't he," commented Lawson. I knew he was referring to Uyeki. "I wonder who spilled the beans."

It almost didn't matter. The die was cast. The trek back to the cave was filled with foreboding. The long shadows of evening wrapped themselves around us in strange and dark ways, as we stumbled down the side of the mountain, barely speaking, gathered in somber thought. Uyeki was after us;

Jose Maria Lacambra

there was little doubt about it now. The manhunt was on and we were the prey. I felt my grip suddenly tightening around the carbine's stock.

180

15. MANHUNT

"I'm going barmy, just sitting around doing nothin' all day," commented Lawson, after the umpteenth game of 'Go'. We'd been playing the oriental version of Checkers since dawn, and were quickly reaching the saturation point. "What'cha say we reconnoiter the approaches."

"We'd better just stick to the cave," I answered. "I'm as bored as you are but I'd hate to be caught out in the open if the Japs were to turn up unexpectedly."

"The monkey'll warn us soon enough," said Lawson. "You couldn't ask for a better sentry."

He was referring to the resident monkey in the huge Lauan tree overhanging the cave. It guarded its territory zealously, ears twitching and swiveling to detect any absence of silence, pausing between swings to screech nervously at any snapping twig or jungle fowl scurrying under the mat of ferns below.

"He reminds me of one of those Roman geese that started honking the alarm any time someone tried tugging at the

Vestals' vests," he added, refusing to let up on his sense of humor.

"Some Vestals!" I answered, morosely. "More like a pair of hunkering rabbits, I'd say! Besides, the monkey's squeals would come too late to do us any good."

So we sat near the cave entrance, whiling away the boring hours playing some more 'Go', growing increasingly frustrated by the forced inactivity.

The lengthening afternoon shadows had started wrapping themselves around the trees outside when we first heard a dog baying in the distance. The monkey's staccato squeals suddenly pierced the cascade's monotone outside, its shrill territorial aggressiveness warning us of approaching visitors.

Peering searchingly through the waterfall's blurring mists, I detected a suspicious movement in the undergrowth which lined the footpath leading to the pool. Several figures, trudging Indian file, soon loomed into view. I recognized, with a start, the familiar tan uniforms and brown leggings of Japanese Army issue.

"Japs!" I whispered hoarsely to Lawson. "They've tracked us down!"

"Uh, oh!" he answered in a small voice. "I guess we're in for a spot of bother."

Moments later I saw a bloodhound tugging at the leash of the platoon's point soldier, its bloodcurdling howls and manic yelps now clearly audible above the dull roar of the falls. Caught up in the excitement of the hunt, the troops un-slung their rifles and crouched behind the underbrush, momentarily disappearing from sight.

The siege was on!

There must have been half a dozen soldiers sprawled around the pool, their leader shouting unintelligible orders at them. Even in the gathering dusk, we could glimmer the dull glint of bayonets as the soldiers affixed them to the barrels of their long rifles. The hound had stopped yelping by now; it was probably munching on its reward for sniffing us out.

"Never thought I'd ever be on the receiving end of those nasty bayonets!" whispered Lawson, as if speaking in hushes could, somehow, delay discovery, perhaps even throw the besiegers off our track. I noticed that his eyes were wide with concern, his freckles now highlighting a blanched expression. We knew, all too well, how deftly they could handle those bayonets.

Though sprawled out in the underbrush around the pool, the soldiers had not fooled the monkey. Its screeching protest had continued undiminished until, suddenly, a rifle shot rang out in the startled afternoon. After absorbing the last reverberation of the report, the forest settled back to its placid sounds of falling water and nighting birds.

"They got the monkey! Must'a brought along a sharpshooter!" I observed ominously. "We'd better keep a low profile."

The eerie quiet was suddenly splintered by the blaring sounds of a human voice.

"Attention!" squawked the voice in hollow, resounding notes, as if through a megaphone. "We know you there inside cave. You surrounded. Come out with hands up!" The barked orders had a familiar Japanese urgency about them.

Speechless, Lawson and I looked at each other, gripped by a mindless terror. It was hard to think coherently, confronted by a platoon of soldiers intent on subtracting us from among the ranks of the living.

"I don't think these bleeders take any prisoners," said Lawson, overwhelmed by his own bleak revelation.

"I don't remember seeing any trucked back during the Iloilo siege," I answered. "I don't think giving up is even an option. It's either putting up our dukes or sneaking out the back door."

"Wonder how long we can hold them off," Lawson asked.

"A couple of clips worth each, maybe," I answered, somberly. "That's all we've got. Wish I knew if Antonio's guerrillas are even coming to help us."

"Not if their families are being held hostage, or something," answered Lawson. "I know hounds are good but not this good. They must have twisted somebody's arm to point them in the right direction. To tell the truth, I half expected Antonio's voice coming through that squawk box. "

"Let's keep 'em occupied for a while," I proposed. "At least till it gets dark. If the guerrillas don't turn up, we can slip out of that hole in the back and make a run for it after dark. It's almost full moon. That should help."

"We've got to get rid of that dog, somehow," said Lawson. "It'll track us down no matter where we go."

"Not if we wade up the stream for a while," I answered. "Water erases human scent, kind'a" I added, remembering how it worked for escaped convicts in the movies.

Our conversation was once more interrupted by the booming sound of the megaphone.

"You have three minutes to come out! After that, you die!" said the voice, with ominous urgency.

I couldn't tell why, but the voice sounded familiar this time around, almost like Uyeki's, with a nose cold. A shiver ran down my back, more because of the voice than its threat.

Rising suddenly from his concealed position behind the cave opening, Lawson stuck his head out of the cave entrance to make sure his voice carried through the roar of the cascade.

"Bollocks!" he shouted insanely.

His outburst caught me completely by surprise. From the stunned silence outside, I sensed that the besiegers were equally surprised, even if all they understood was the indignant tone of the juvenile dare.

Yanking on his shirt, I pulled Lawson down to the ground beside me. "That was dumb!" I said, still startled by his outcry. "Now they really know we're here, you pimple head!"

My outrage was cut short when someone outside issued a hoarse command. The order was followed almost instantly by a volley of rifle fire. A dozen bullets whined past us, ricocheting around the cave. Lawson and I hugged the ground behind the cave entrance, hands wrapped around the back of our heads, instinctively adopting the fetal position, aware of how suddenly life could cease.

"Holy Jesus!" muttered Lawson from somewhere behind his elbows, more out of threatened endurance than piety. "These buggers are really serious!"

"Let's shoot back. That'll give them something to think about," I said, slithering toward the two carbines that we'd propped up by the wall on the far side of the cave.

"Yeah!" said Lawson excitedly. "It may even buy us some time for the guerrillas to come help."

"Or for it to get dark and help us escape, if they don't," I said, handing him a rifle.

Disengaging their safety latches, we pointed the weapons in the general direction of the pool outside and opened fire with two or three shots apiece. The noise inside the cave was deafening. Before the din had subsided, we heard the sinister sound of bullets whizzing past us, followed closely by the cracks of several reports outside.

The duel had been joined. There was no turning back now. Firing back at the Japanese troops had been a fateful decision. We had graduated, almost unwittingly, from the status of truant children eluding capture, to that of full-fledged combatants. The realization that we were now the enemy overwhelmed me. After all those bedtime stories, I, too, had burned my ships and drawn my own line in the sand.

"Time's on our side," I said, hopefully. "I don't believe they're gonna assault us in the dark, do you?"

"Yeah," whispered Lawson. "They'll probably wait till daybreak. I certainly would, if I had to walk on those slippery rocks outside, Indian file, while being shot at, point blank!"

"We're down to one clip of ammunition each," I said, after a lull in the conversation. "We'd better ease up on the shooting until nightfall."

"Or until the cavalry comes to the rescue," said Lawson.

"Fat chance!"

Suddenly, there was a dull sound of a metallic object bouncing around the cave. We heard it roll toward the rear of the cave, followed, moments later, by a sheet of brilliant flame that exploded violently in the bowels of the cave. The deafening roar that followed rang in our ears with excruciating pain. Swirling dust, mingled with the smell of gunpowder, made breathing difficult.

Dazed by the grenade blast, but otherwise unhurt, we instinctively fired several shots, as if to warn the enemy that danger still lurked within, trying to discourage any thought of unchallenged assault.

Sensing that we might not emerge unscathed from the next grenade, we decided that it was time to execute our escape plan.

"Let's go!" I motioned to Lawson toward the bowels of the cave. Spraying the pool area with the last of our ammunition, we rushed to the back of the cave. Taking the right fork, we groped our way along the dark, narrowing passage, until we reached the large boulder that almost obstructed further progress. We then squeezed ourselves through, to the far side of the dislodged rock.

"There's bound to be more grenades coming soon. Let's wait a while till the next one goes off before climbing out," I suggested, afraid we'd get hit by shrapnel while climbing the boulder.

No sooner had I spoken than the sound of metal bouncing farther up the passageway, reached us. We had just enough time to crouch behind the large boulder, cover our ears with our hands and open our mouths wide.

The roar that followed was like a thousand firecrackers going off simultaneously, right next to our ears. The gust from the blast was like a funneled typhoon forcing air out of the tunnel through the narrow opening directly above us. Molten pieces of steel ricocheted off the walls around us, falling at our feet like hot lava pellets. We gasped for air, coughing and choking on the explosion's fumes and dislodged dust, eardrums throbbing with exquisite pain.

Recovering briefly from the shock of the blast, I grabbed Lawson by the arm and pointed at the opening above us. It was too dark for him to see my gesture, and talking was of little use in our momentary deafness. But we both instinctively knew what to do before the next grenade was lobbed into the cave.

Still in a daze, we managed to pull ourselves together, fumbling our way up the boulder. We could see the stars through the opening above. I helped Lawson up the slippery rock, pulling myself up right behind him. With not a moment to spare, I heaved Lawson up through the hole and, leveraging my feet on the gnarled root system, yanked myself up, right behind him.

No sooner had I cleared the cavity than a reddish flash punched through from under it, briefly lighting the darkness around us with a web of ruddy light. The blast that followed was like a muffled burp in the earth's gut. The ground shook convulsively under me, just before the whoosh of the grenade's blast came rushing through the opening, ruffling the tall ferns around us in ever expanding ripples.

"That was one close call!" I whispered hoarsely, shuddering at the thought of what a second's delay would have meant. We lay there on the ferns for a few moments, drained of all emotion, uncaring almost. There was no monkey above us to protest the nocturnal disturbance. The sharpshooter may have done us a favor. Now, only a full moon, shimmering in a star-sundered sky, bore witness to the unfolding drama below. It looked so peaceful up there and yet death kept ripping the bowels of the earth beneath us, every few minutes.

"We've gotta go," urged Lawson. "I think I hear voices outside the cave entrance below. Looks like they're getting ready for one of those Banzai charges they've been practicing for, all these past months."

The sobering thought cleared away any remaining cobwebs, spurring us into action. Creeping down to the rushing water, we started wading upstream in it. It was the only way we knew to throw the bloodhound off our scent. For our ruse to work, we had to interpose as much watery distance between our entry point and our final exit from the river, wherever that may be, and do it with great urgency.

We struggled against the shallow, whitewater current, slipping and stumbling on the smooth, algae-covered rocks. Sloshing through the moon-drenched river, we panted uphill at a bruising pace. The cool night air lent a welcome relief to the forced, sodden march. The river's pools and small cascades were hard to negotiate, particularly when the overhang above shut out the already faltering moonlight. As if surprised by the strange intrusion, the night noises would hush in a pocket of forest immediately surrounding us, a hundred eyes and ears nervously straining to track our progress in the dappled light.

It was during one of these lulls of nocturnal sound that we first heard the bloodhound's distant yelps. We'd been travelling for about an hour and had progressed no more than a mile from the cave. Although the dog had surely lost our scent at our entry point in the river, our evading maneuver must have been all too obvious. The Japanese were simply coming upstream, following their instincts rather than the dog's sense of smell.

"They're coming!" I said needlessly. "We've gotta get out of this river. It's too slow going in it."

"Wish it were deeper," answered Lawson, cryptically.

"How would that help?"

"We could submerge ourselves in some deep pool or something. Maybe even breathe through a hollow reed until they've gone away," he explained. There was no hint of his usual humor under stress. The ragged logic of the scheme told me that Lawson was as desperate as I.

Meanwhile, the baying of the approaching hound grew louder, unraveling what little coherence our escape plan might have originally had.

"I tell you what," I proposed, grasping at no sturdier straws than his. "We can't leave the water or the dog will sniff us out. What we need is an overhanging bough to climb up on. Keep an eye out for one."

As if in answer to our prayer, a stout limb from a large acacia tree dipped low over the stream, several hundred yards upstream, almost obstructing our path. Pulling ourselves up on it, we quickly clambered up the hefty trunk to its higher branches. From somewhere above us, a startled owl whirred off, hooting its surprise in a blur of flapping wings.

It took us several minutes to reach the tree's loftiest limbs, sprawling out high above the river. From there, we surveyed the landscape below us. The stream was like a gash, slashing through the vegetation. The forest's moon-dappled canopy spread out below us, serenely indifferent to the anguish of survival being enacted in its midst.

We could hear voices below us now, framed by the yelps of the confused bloodhound. Shouted commands wafted up to us, a guttural urgency masking their displeasure at having been given the slip by a younger, more cunning prey. Lawson and I held our breath to better sense the enemy's position and progress in the darkness below. We could now see several tiny circles of light swaying back and forth along both edges of the brook, as their flashlights' owners progressed upstream, methodically combing the rugged terrain.

"There'll be hell to pay if he comes back empty handed," I whispered sarcastically, as I watched the last trooper's circle of light disappear from view. The hound was still howling, as if trying to bolster its handler's confidence.

"We'll be O.K. so long as that mutt keeps barking and those beggars keep walking upstream," commented Lawson, relieved at the fortunate turn of events.

Several minutes passed before the forest reverted to its nocturnal noises. There was no sign of the Japanese anywhere.

"I think we ought'a double back on our tracks while the Japs are heading in the wrong direction," I proposed. That maneuver had served us well in our endless Cowboys and Indians games of what now seemed eons ago. In evasive tactics, the unexpected had, more times than not, been the most fruitful approach.

"What if they left a sentry or two hanging around the cave area, waiting for the rest to come back?" asked Lawson worriedly.

"We could end-run them. It's not the soldiers we gotta worry about. It's that dog, and he's headed the wrong way now. Look, if we're gonna do it, it's gotta be quick, before those Japs come back," I said, trying to lend some urgency to the latest change in our escape plan.

"O.K." mumbled Lawson halfheartedly, still unconvinced of the wisdom of leaving the safety of the tree for a risky jump into the unknown.

"Where are we headed for, anyway?" he asked, as we started climbing down the tree.

"I'm not sure, but it can't be back to Jordan. That'd be like walking into the lion's den. Besides, we've probably gotten those people down there into a heap of trouble already."

"I've been thinking," I said, after dropping to the ground. "Perhaps it's best to head on down toward the eastern seaboard. What do you think?"

"Smashing! Surely there aren't any Japs there, at least not for now," said Lawson, jumping off the low-hanging limb onto the river bank.

We didn't bother trying to cover our tracks this time around. Slogging our way downriver would have made painfully slow going, and time was now of the essence; it was hard enough hiking by moonlight. We approached the waterfalls stealthily, making a long detour around the pool in case the Japanese had posted sentries around the cave. We went back into the stream beyond it, farther downhill, just in case the hound doubled back and picked up our scent again.

Descending the mountain in a generally easterly direction was new territory for us but we knew that, sooner or later, the stream we were wading in would eventually lead us down to the eastern seaboard. We abandoned the stream after a while, bushwhacking it for several pathless miles. Fed by a growing number of tributaries, the gurgling stream had grown perceptibly wider, until it had now become a full-fledged river, hungering for the sea.

It was still dark when we approached a hamlet that rested sleepily on the fork of two mountain trails. A cock crowed in the distance, with confused hopes of dawn. From some sleepy courtyard, a dog of nameless breed barked an alarm, which several other mongrels picked up unconvincingly, lending depth to the silence of the night.

"I'm sure glad it's not that perishing bloodhound we left behind!" whispered Lawson, as we circled the hamlet, giving it wide berth. And then there was silence again, broken only by an occasional owl hoot, framed by a myriad of toad croaks.

It must have been close to three in the morning. I estimated that we had trudged no more than four or five miles, as the crow flies, since we climbed down from the tree. Our feet and legs were badly bruised from the merciless pace along rocks and brambles. But despite the exhaustion, it was still not yet time to rest.

"Must be another three or four miles to the sea," I guessed. "This dirt path we're now on is headed due east. I think it'll lead us to that coastal barrio we spotted from the peaks coupl'a days ago."

"I believe you're right," said Lawson. "It's gonna be easy going from here on out." I could tell he was as tired as I.

A doubting blush in the eastern sky hinted at the approaching dawn. Soon, we reached an unpaved road running along the island's eastern seaboard. Half a mile to the south, a village slumbered fitfully, trying to ignore the tentative chirps and crows of the awakening December morning. Exhausted from the night-long trek, drained of all emotion, too tired to even care how far behind we'd left the hound of death, we pressed on against the gathering light, dragging ourselves the remaining distance to a deserted beach.

Like disoriented lemmings, we shuffled over to the edge of the water and plopped ourselves down on the shallows. With the gentle smallness of the young tide, the wavelets lapping about us staved off sleep for a while. But soon, the sea would recede from under us, leaving us on the sloping sand, like two stranded porpoises in deep slumber.

16. JUAN

The sun was almost overhead, unsuccessfully trying to awaken us with its shards of angry light. A curious crowd had gathered around us, and it was their repressed voices that finally broke through my consciousness. Eyes still shut, I could hear them talking in hushes, puzzling over the strange gifts the sea had deposited on their lonely beach during the night.

The words '*patáy*' and '*buhî*' were being exchanged, in respectful argument as to whether we were alive or dead. Someone gently laid his hand on my jugular as if to settle the argument. I opened my eyes and saw, through the blear of sleep, a dozen eyes peering down on me. Almost in unison, the crowd drew back, surprised.

"*Ay abaw, mabuhî silá!*" they gasped as one, as if the fact that we were alive required communal confirmation.

I sat up slowly, and prodded Lawson to wake up.

"*Sinó camó?*" asked an old man in the crowd, wanting to know who we were. His rough, sun-furrowed face spoke of a lifetime spent harvesting the bountiful sea. His warm black eyes crinkled with the curiosity of one who had lived long enough to know that the sea sometimes yields strange and unexpected offerings.

In a mixture of Visayâ and English, I explained our background and predicament, as I'd done with Antonio, almost a month earlier. Yes, they had heard of the Japanese landing two days earlier in Jordan, across the island, to the West. Bad news travels fast. The crowd understood most of my story, listening, spellbound, to a strange tale that almost beggared belief. Lawson pitched in whenever my mouth dried or the story lagged.

The children, especially, were mesmerized by our tale, letting out '*abaw's!*' of awe and delight, during our account. Their faces turned somber as the story drew to its dramatic close, with the Japanese in hot pursuit only a few hours earlier.

"*Magutom kami. Gusto kami magkaon,*" I said when I had come to the end of the account, telling them that we were hungry and could use some food.

There was a sudden flurry of huddled discussion amongst them. They argued over us, each wanting to feed and house us. The old fisherman finally convinced them that he should take us under his wing. He lived alone, he argued, and there was nobody else but an old man to suffer the consequences of harboring the 'enemy,' in the unlikely event that the Japanese sniffed us out. Reluctantly, the rest agreed.

The group formed around us as we walked toward the village, the men gripping the handles of the sheathed *binangon* machetes that hung loosely from their belts. The mood grew

197

festive as we approached the small village. The children ran on ahead of the committee, announcing the news with peals of laughter and growing merriment.

"Anong baryo itó?" I asked the old fisherman, curious to know the name of the village we were approaching.

"Suclaran," he answered with a certain note of pride.

The news of our arrival had spread like wildfire throughout the village, by the time we reached the first nipa huts on the outskirts of the coastal settlement. Women and children leaned out of their windows to stare at the two tanned European boys in torn, sun-bleached clothes. Some of them had never seen foreigners before, and the sight of two young live ones spat out by the sea, like human driftwood onto their midst, was something to ogle because they were going to talk about it for many moons to come.

The crowd grew as we progressed down the village's main street, children elbowing and pushing to position themselves nearer us. Caught up in the mounting excitement, mangy dogs barked out at no one in particular, while chickens scurried out of harm's way. Several small black pigs, wallowing in mud holes by the road, added to the noise with their disgruntled oinks.

"It's starting to look like a bleeding parade," commented Lawson, bemused by all the excitement. "They're gonna have a ruddy time keeping us a secret after all this hullabaloo."

We eventually reached the old man's home, where the brief procession came to an end. Untrimmed gumamela bushes grew helter-skelter in the small, weed-choked garden, gracing it with their unexpected touches of bright red hibiscus blossoms. Plants grew randomly, where seeds had fallen in the uncontrived garden. Despite the obvious lack of attention, small lettuce heads and gangly tomato vines grew in a vegetable plot in the backyard. Drying in the sun, a dozen mullet halves hung stiffly from a wire strung between rows of beanstalks, permeating the yard with the pungent smell of the sea. Tied to a stake, the inevitable fighting cock pecked dispiritedly at grains of rice strewn about it.

Closer to the beach, majestic palm trees grew crookedly, leaning to seaward, hungering for the salty breeze, as if sensing that facing the sea was their only chance of surviving the frequent storms that whipped these isles. A hammock was slung between two neighboring palms, and just beyond, a small *parao* sat on the beach, its bright patterned sails furled neatly at its prow.

The crowd, which had thronged about us, as if expecting a speech or a jig from the young foreigners, appeared disappointed when our host turned to them and asked them, in a kind voice, to go back to their homes. He reasoned that we were worn out and hungry and in need of rest after the harrowing night.

The group soon thinned out until, finally, only the three of us remained, standing in front of the hut. The mention of food alone had driven shafts of hunger through Lawson and me. We suspected that the old man was no Malíng at the kitchen, but even a bowl of rice would taste wonderful, not having eaten in over a day.

We climbed the rickety ladder that led up to the hut's entrance. Even before setting foot inside, I knew that it would be like the one we'd slept in during our first night in Guimarás. I guessed right. The fisherman's single-room abode was simply furnished. You could tell, from the general disarray inside, that no woman lived there. Soiled plates and unclean pans lay about, and the bed in the corner was undone. I knew we were going to enjoy living there.

"My name is Juan," the old fisherman announced with serene formality, motioning us to sit at the table in the middle of the room. Ambling over to an ancient stove sitting stolidly in the far corner of the room, he rummaged for matches to start a fire.

"You are welcome to my humble abode," he continued in a soft, even voice. "I live alone, as you can see. I pish for a living. I hab lived in Guimarás all my lipe and know the small islands around here like the back of my hand. In these unsettled times, the sea is saper than the land. I hab a pairly large *parao* and you will sail with me tomorrow."

It was good to have someone else making decisions for us again. The harrowing choices of the previous night could fill anyone's lifetime hunger for plucky judgments and gritty decisions. Juan was just what the doctor had ordered for two tired and bewildered pilgrims. Too much adventure can leech away some of the rashness and daring from even young and restless spirits.

Juan fixed us some rice with *sugpó*. We devoured the boiled shrimp, using our fingers to roll up the sticky rice into bite-sized morsels. Juan looked on benignly, picking at his plate disinterestedly. When we had finished the simple but nourishing course, Juan sliced a pineapple for desert and watched it promptly disappear in a blur of drooling sounds and slurping gulps. One of the delights of going native was being able to ignore table manners without motherly reprimands.

"I had children once," Juan said wistfully, a smile permanently etched in his craggy face. "They never had your appetite, though."

"What happened to them?" Lawson asked, nibbling around the pineapple core.

"They grew up," he answered briefly. I had noticed that men of the sea tend to be sparse with words. It must be all that living alone on a fickle sea, half expecting to end one's days in some sudden squall or howling typhoon. Their stark existence must teach them to make do with only the bare essentials of life, even in speech.

"Today you rest," said the old man, getting up from the table. His terse command brought back childhood memories of nannies ordering us to bed for the siesta. Only this time the order was welcome. It was only mid afternoon but we were too exhausted to do otherwise.

"Tomorrow at dawn, we sail," he said, heading for the door. He knew we'd be sleeping till then.

17. THE ENCHANTED ISLES

The sun was peeking over Mt. Kanlaón as we dragged the *parao* down to the water's edge, early the next morning. Shoving the sailboat into the becalmed sea, we clambered aboard and helped Juan hoist the sail up the mainmast. A feeble land breeze flirted with the varicolored sail briefly, and then started filling out the canvas in earnest, tugging at the nimble *parao* until its ropes creaked and its rig groaned. The stumpy bowsprit sniffed the air tentatively on a southerly tack to leeward.

It was a glorious feeling to be at sea again and sense the freedom of heading out in any direction along its vast, wet highways to nowhere. Lawson and I sat near the prow, gulping lungfuls of salt air, feet dangling by the side, feeling the bow wave leap up to meet us with its arch of curling spray. The breeze on my face had a cleansing, soothing quality about it.

I observed Juan sitting at the tiller and envied his being able to roam, anytime he chose, the bold uncharted openness of the sea. Nose raised slightly, as if sniffing the compass-less void, his private vision seemed to take him far beyond the gentle swells of the Visayan seas, to some uncharted isles, unreachable by direct intent. He had sailed alone so many years that company now would not readily alter his own inner sounds and solitary rhythms.

No one spoke for a long time, each one wrapped in his own thoughtful peace, the old man dreaming dreams, the boys conjuring visions. An hour went by before we first detected land formations ahead of us. The large neighboring island of Negros loomed out of the sea to the southeast, its tall volcano rising proudly above the mists, draped in the purplish tinge of featureless distance.

"Pulupandan," said Juan, motioning with his head toward the large island's westernmost tip. I gazed on the land's end with nostalgia. That had been the La Carlota sugar plantation's harbor, where Dad and I used to fly into, sometimes, on the small Sikorsky seaplane.

"Dad and I used to visit there often with Fritz Kauffman, before the war. It feels like worlds ago now!" I commented.

I suddenly felt a need to cry without knowing why. From the labyrinth of youthful memories emerged the time I wept when Mom and Dad came to pick me up from Pilar, the year before the war. I had spent a wonderful summer vacation there with the Aranas, but it was good to go back home again. I remembered how letting go like that had made me feel a little silly but relieved, at the same time. I had puzzled many times over the reverse alchemy of turning happiness into tears.

"I wonder how Mom and Dad are doing," said Lawson wistfully. "It's been almost a month, hasn't it?"

The timing of his question was uncanny, almost as if he'd been reading my thoughts.

"About," I answered. "They chased us out of San Agustin around the middle of November. Christmas must be right around the corner."

"It's gonna be my first Christmas away from home," I reflected. That made me feel a little sorry for myself. "Jesus Jimenez and Angel Arana are probably taking the crèche Christ child around the parish right about now." I smiled, thinking of Jesus Jimenez roaming the streets in dubious piety, red robes billowing and surplice flapping in the breeze.

We sailed south for at least a couple of hours on a steady course before the two tiny islets that had bobbed in and out of view, finally acquired presence and resolution. Even after we were finally upon them, they still remained diminutive, like two enchanted isles on a green sea, with their thatch of palms swaying tremulously in the wind. The aquamarine water lapped placidly at the hard-packed coral sand of their beaches. If one could dream of paradise, the scene came close to a waking description of it.

"The nearest one is Nadulao," said Juan, breaking the magic spell. "The one just beyond is Nalunga. The larger one, even farther south is Inampulugan. We're exactly midway between Guimarás and Negros." Pausing for a moment, he continued: "We can't see it yet but just behind Nadulao, here, is a tiny islet, a rock, really. Doesn't eben have a name. Pew people know it, but in the narrow strait between it and Nadulao are the best pishing grounds in the whole wide world."

Lawson and I looked at each other, amazed to hear Juan actually speaking in sentences. That was the longest monologue he had uttered since we met. Not surprisingly, the subject had been maritime. He was in his element now. A subtle transformation seemed to have come over him, as if something from within had just lit up the sad, knowing eyes, washing away the creases from his furrowed face. He was almost jubilant, in anticipation of casting the net.

As we eased into the narrow strait he had just described, the wind started blowing around us in erratic whorls, as it funneled fitfully between the two islets. Juan had gotten up from his seat by then, and was starting to pay his net out, all the while maneuvering the *parao* expertly in a wide, unerring circle. He tacked only once before catching up eventually with the bobbing net floater he had dropped at the beginning of the maneuver, neatly closing the fish trap.

"Look at all the fish!" cried Lawson. "There must be a hundred of them in there!"

Seething in the depths of the encircling net, a myriad of nondescript fish thrashed about in a ferment of distress. The churning waters erupted suddenly in a furious patch of frenzied fish, startled mullet leaping high in the air as if sensing imminent capture.

"Wow! I never saw anything like it before!" I remarked, sensing a quickening of the pulse at the very thought of hauling in the gleanings of the rich sea harvest.

The old man skipped about jauntily in the *parao*, dashing from bow to stern, giving orders, hauling up the slack in the net with a nimbleness that belied his age. It occurred to me that the surge of adrenalin that comes from hauling in fish must be as ancient as man, and wondered why the expression 'joy of the hunt' didn't have an analogous 'joy of the fish.'

We saw only one other *parao* all day, sailing furtively in the distance. Juan had latched on to that uncharted glory hole of fish that no one else seemed to know about and, like all sly fishermen, wasn't about to tell. Several times during the day, Lawson and I dove into the green ocean to cool off, once having to scramble back into the boat when Juan warned us of a small hammerhead cruising lazily nearby.

The large water well in the center of the boat's hull was almost full when we hauled in the day's last catch, late in the afternoon. We had barely moved from the same spot all day, and yet the bounty of the sea was evident in its motley offering of *bangús* and mullet, shrimp and *tangingue*, sardines and *lapu lapu*, slithering against each other in the fish well, with resigned fin strokes.

We knew it was getting on six o'clock when we finally left the happy fishing grounds, because the 'Lone Ranger' was, just then, flying overhead on its casual evening reconnaissance of the Visayan Islands. Lawson and I waved at it frantically, but the pilot didn't acknowledge our greeting. Juan gave us a puzzled look but said nothing. Expertly, he nosed the boat in a southerly tack toward Nalunga.

We sailed around the diminutive islet, its pristine coral beach wrapping the mile long island's coast in a dream of white sand.

"It's uninhabited," Juan said. "I usually spend the night here rather than in Nadulao. There's more pirewood here. And, for some reason, also pewer mosquitos."

After landing on its southern beach, we pulled the *parao* up to the high tide weed mark. We then built a lean-to out of palm leaves, and then set out to gather driftwood for the fire. Before it turned dark, we were eating rice with grilled *tanginge* mackerel. Its meat was white and tender, terse with freshness.

"Tan-gin-ge," I said out loud, giving each syllable a metered pause. I loved the sound of the name itself; it hinted at speed. "Fastest fish in the world," I added, remembering something I'd read in a large blue Geography textbook, years earlier. In my mind's eye I could still see Uyeki's baroque calligraphy on the ex-libris affixed to its first page. I quickly shoved the unpleasant thought out of mind.

Lawson and I decided to explore the tiny island, after supper. We left Juan sitting under a palm tree, puffing blissfully on a conical stogie, not unlike the ones Alíng Andáng, the washer woman, used to roll. We walked slowly along the narrow strip of beach that encircled the islet, its white, hard-packed sand reflecting the moonlight in soft and tenuous ways. Sand crabs scurried from our path in a blur of sideways motion, their stalked eyes swiveling nervously after us.

The night air was warm despite the lateness of the year. Unpretentious wavelets lapped rhythmically at the shoreline. We took a dip in the becalmed waters and came out smelling of the sharp edge of the sea. In the time it took us to circle the little island, the heavens had blossomed, star by star. We found Juan still up when we returned to the lean-to.

"They've landed in Mindoro," he said, clear out of the blue. The unexpected news was like summer thunder in clear air. "That's either good news or bad news por us," he added.

I knew exactly what he meant. The good part was that Mindoro was closer to Panay than Leyte, the first landing site. That meant that the Americans, who'd been bogged down in Leyte, were finally on the move again. The disheartening part was that Mindoro already lay to the north of us, signaling that we'd been bypassed, as Antonio had once darkly hinted.

"When did you find out?" I asked, puzzled at the delayed revelation.

"Radio in Suclaran, yesterday, while you slept. Armed Porces Network broadcast."

"Think they might swing south and land in Panay next?" asked Lawson, more as a plea than a query. "After all, Mindoro's no more'n a hundred miles from here."

"Don't think so," he answered briefly. Juan belonged to that breed of men who prefer rejoicing at disproved omens than regretting unfulfilled hopes.

Even in the moonlight, Lawson looked crestfallen. "Sounds like we're in it for the long haul, then," he commented, dejectedly. "The bleeder's heading north! Gone off and left us!" he mumbled in disgust. "I kind'a suspected this would happen. Felt it in my bones all along. Ruddy windbag!"

Juan regarded Lawson with an air of tolerance, in the wise and understanding way of age. "No sense worrying about things you can't control," he said evenly. After a pause, he added: "Whether they liberate us bepore or apter Tokyo, war will soon be ober."

"Hope we'll be there to tell it," said Lawson, dejectedly.

"You will," said Juan with calm conviction. "Wars come and wars go, but young boys prevail. I was your age when we pought the Spaniards and then the Americans in '98. This one, too, will pass."

I'd never actually known anyone who'd fought with Aguinaldo. I'd always thought the combatants of that ancient war were long dead and buried. In the light of the dying campfire Juan looked, and even sounded, like my idea of an oracle. Strangely, his words of calm wisdom compelled hope.

That night, Lawson and I lay on the palm leaves we'd strewn over the warm sand. The sky above bore the pricks of a million pins of light in resigned, majestic silence. Gazing at the crater-smudged moon directly above us, it occurred to me that it was also shining on our home in Iloilo, not more than twenty miles away, as a guardian angel flies. Thoughts of home were now recurring with renewed insistence. I could even dimly glimmer the joyous scene of our return. There wouldn't be fatted calves to kill but there'd be plenty of laughs and hugs to make up for their lack. There'd also be plenty of questions to answer about the not so empty days in Guimarás.

18. THE PARTY

We sailed before first light the next day. Like all fishermen worth their salt, Juan knew that the first one in with the sea harvest would command the highest prices at the marketplace. A hint of a Northwesterly blowing in the young morning forced us to tack several times before clearing Nadulong and heading out for the open sea, on the northward leg to Suclaran.

Flying fish glided by effortlessly, defying gravity with their improbable long distance gliding. Schools of dolphin swam playfully alongside the *parao*, showing off their watery acrobatics. Their playfulness always seemed at its most whimsical around dawn.

Suclaran Bay came into view, several hours later. Juan maneuvered the boat expertly toward a stretch of sandy beach along which villagers had already started to gather; it was, probably, near the marketplace. No sooner had we beached the *parao* than a small crowd started milling around us, appraising the first catch of the day. The presence of the two foreign kids aboard only added to the small spectacle.

The bidding that followed was lively. Expert eyes ascertained the quality and quantity of the catch at a glance, even before the different species had been culled and counted. Lump sum offers were made for the lot and the deal was closed before we even realized that a business transaction had been under way; as in the fish market at Jordan, no currency changed hands. The barter system was in effect here too, with only the spoken word and a handshake to close the deal.

Two elderly women deftly separated the fish according to size and type, tossing them onto separate shallow wicker trays which they covered with banana leaves. Heaving the trays up onto the rolled bandanas atop their heads, they whisked them off to market.

I thought it odd that most of the crowd followed us to Juan's house. A group of children elbowed their way through the grownups, ogling us with unabashed curiosity, as if reluctant to miss any sound or movement from the two young foreigners who'd sailed in from some strange and distant land.

"These are the town elders," said Juan, nodding towards a small group of townsfolk that had gathered in front of his hut, as we approached it. "It's probably a reception committee to welcome you two boys oppicially."

A short, bowlegged man with a pockmarked face, dressed in a starched Barong Tagalog shirt, edged his way to the front of the group and took control of the proceedings. Despite his awkward English, he spoke in a voice which drew everyone's attention.

"Welcome to Suclaran," he said, somewhat belatedly. "The tales op your exploits hab preceded you. You may be young in age but we hear you hab the hearts op men. We are proud op you and commend you por your bravery."

He paused for effect before adding: "The town Council has unanimously agreed to name you honorary citizens of Suclaran." So saying, he raised himself up on his tiptoes, laid a wreath of pungent *Ilang-Ilang* blossoms around our necks and gave us each a hearty hug.

The small group of people that had gathered around us wished us long life, starting a round of applause with scattered shouts of *"Mabuhay ang batáan!"* Self-consciously, the town elders lined up to shake our hands with awkward formality. The less bashful patted us on the shoulder, beaming with frank admiration.

While we'd been out fishing, news of our run-in with the Japanese in the mountains had been confirmed by someone who arrived from Jordan the day before. He had brought back news of brazen exploits in the mountain fastnesses near there, where two foreign kids had held off the Japanese army and vanished without a trace. The boys had even managed to wound an officer in the process, the story went.

Lawson and I looked at each other, wondering whether to bask in the sunny interval or start worrying about the consequences of the wounding, if it had, indeed, occurred.

"Are they still in Guimarás?" I asked, worried about all the fuss. "Was anyone hurt in Jordan?" I pursued.

"Hindî!" they piped up in negative unison.

Lawson and I were relieved, but a little embarrassed by all the attention. We just stood there stiffly, smiling silly grins, trying unsuccessfully to explain that it wasn't bravery at all, just survival instinct, pure and simple.

They would have none of it. Legends, once started, are hard to squelch. As the afternoon wore on, the aura surrounding us grew in intensity until, by dusk, the myth had turned into unquestioned truth in the minds of these fishermen. We had become reluctant heroes, overnight.

Someone, meanwhile, had started roasting a suckling pig on a spit in Juan's backyard. The basting aroma pervaded the neighborhood like a burnt and delicious offering. Spread out on makeshift tables inside the hut was enough food to feed the multitudes.

Women smiled demurely as they fussed over Lawson and me, clucking with maternal solicitude. Every family had brought us some small token of their esteem and hospitality. By nightfall, Lawson and I were decked out in fancy Barong Tagalog shirts, ill fitting shorts and floppy rubber-soled sandals.

"You look weird in clean clothes," said Lawson. "A little 'keedlish,' kind'a."

"Eat your heart out, Davies," I said smugly, pleased with my new outfit.

Late in the afternoon, the women started serving a boggling variety of exotic food. Tuba palm wine flowed generously, drowning inhibitions and lightening already giddy spirits. When it turned dark, Chinese candle lanterns were strung up between the nipa huts and lit, shedding light on the festivities.

A motley group of musicians that went by the unlikely name of 'The Hamelins' turned up at dusk with an odd assortment of guitars, mandolins, trumpets, even a thumping bass drum. The usual discordant warm-up practice notes continued unabated into the night, every bar an insult to harmony. But their lively rhythms more than made up for the dissonance and, before long, everyone in the street was dancing to the phonic disaster.

Lawson and I barely knew how to dance. Our repertoire consisted of a single dance step, the Fox Trot. But that never deterred us. Being the guests of honor, we got to dance nonstop. The young girls in the crowd jostled each other to get the next dance with us. They giggled a lot, probably because our 'Trot' jarred rhythmically with the Rigodón-like tunes which the Hamelins insisted on playing. Or perhaps it was Lawson's peculiar stride, which vaguely resembled a Groucho Marx lope. But our tuba-inspired enthusiasm more than compensated for our graceless dancing.

"Mari Kawayan would'a wet her pants if she saw us now!" commented Lawson as he trotted past me one time, the distraction almost causing him to trip over his giggly partner.

He was enjoying dancing immensely, believing he really could. Under the feeble light of the overhead paper lanterns, I noticed that while his left hand clutched his partner's on high, pumping it up and down rhythmically to some harvest tune, his right hand rested blissfully on her front instead of her back, as propriety suggested. Too bashful to reprove the Scot for his innocent but quaint approach to dancing, his partner's bewildered look bespoke the struggle between outrage and delight.

Meanwhile, the Scottish rite was causing a bit of a stir along the sidelines. The other girls eagerly awaited their turn to learn the novel Nordic dancing technique. I didn't have the heart to pull Lawson aside and point the error of his ways. The puzzled look on his face, when he saw me doubled up with laughter, was an ode to innocence. It was altogether too funny for words.

A merry old time was had by all that evening. It was the biggest party ever thrown in our honor that either of us could recall. Even the Davies' affairs before the war paled in comparison. Swept up by the spell of the exuberant moment, we tried to sweet-talk our dancing partners into moonlit walks along the beach, but their nervous mothers dampened our ardors with riveting hawkeyed glances. They seemed to be particularly vigilant of the freckled one with the not so cherubic blue eyes and the odd hand placement. He may have skirted the Japanese but he was going to remain under their motherly sights so long as their precious wards were up and doing.

I don't remember whether the party finally broke up because the candles in the dangling lanterns finally burned out or whether the musicians got too giddy with Tuba to proceed even with their dubious plinking and tooting.

The bass drummer was the last to leave. Thundering down the empty lane, weaving from side to side of the dirt road, he was followed by several revelers, resolutely staggering after their pie-eyed Hamelin drummer, dead-set on reenacting an old German fairy tale.

The last of the trailing drunks wove his unconscious way into the night, singing an improbable Japanese martial hymn:

"Komo to waku, ajiano chikara ju oku no..."

The drunken strains wafted on the shoulders of the inebriated night for a few moments until someone dropped a flower pot on him.

And then there was silence.

Curled up on our mats that night, just before slipping into sleep, Juan said: "Messenger say the Japanese lept Guimarás yesterday. American planes sank one of their launches on the harbor the day bepore."

I was starting to get used to Juan's impromptu newsbreaks. "Anybody hurt in Jordan?" I asked matter-of-factly.

"No," he responded. "Just a house burned."

I froze at the news. All the night's revelry suddenly slid into a meaningless void. I was sure that it was Antonio's and Mailíng's home that had been scorched by the retreating soldiers. I was sickened by the thought of our adoptive family, now homeless, wandering aimlessly with their young brood. That was a tall price to pay for their generous hospitality towards two perfect strangers.

"Do you know whose house it was?" asked Lawson. I could tell, from his anxious question, that his thoughts were running parallel to mine.

"He didn't say," responded the old man. He would have left it at that had he not sensed our mounting concern. Speaking softly in the dark, he added:

"Life is the most precious thing," he reflected sagely. "Material things can always be replaced, especially nipa huts. We build them in a day," he added reassuringly.

"It was not a nipa hut," I commented dejectedly. "It'll take more than a day to rebuild that house."

"Probably a week, then," he responded equably. "The whole town will turn up one day and pitch in. Community epport."

"Then I think we should go help rebuild it," I said. "It's the least we can do. After all, we may have been the cause of that burning." The brain registered the decision only after the words had been uttered.

"But we don't eben know ip it was your priend's house!" protested the old man. "You should wait a pew days until things settle down. Then I'll take you to Jordan myselp, on the *parao*."

It was obvious that he didn't want us to leave. "We were just starting to know each other," he added, pathetically. "Besides, you've just been made honorary citizens of Suclaran, remember?" His words trembled with righteousness, trying to tap into the roots of duty by gently hinting at the done thing.

"We're honored to be considered one of you," interposed Lawson. "We'll always be thankful for all you've done for us. But Antonio needs our help now. We've gotta go and help him. You've gotta understand."

I couldn't have expressed the basics of the social contract any better. Lawson was right on the mark, as usual.

"Very well, then," said the old man, resignedly. "Let me at least sail you around to Jordan. I have pamily business to tend to on the way there, anyway. If it wasn't your priend's home that got burned, and it is your wish to return to Iloilo, I'll be happy to sail you there too."

I felt moved, yet one more time, by the expression of raw human kindness. Before getting completely choked up, I managed to whisper hoarsely: "Thank you, old man."

"We sail tomorrow, then," said Juan. "It'll take us a day to get to Jordan. We'll spend the night at my niece's place in San Miguel."

19. HOME IS THE SAILOR

Lawson and I readied the boat for the trip the next morning, while Juan was in town, purchasing last minute provisions. News of our unexpected departure had spread around the village, and people were soon turning up at the beach, to see us off. Even the girls we'd danced with the night before were there, with *Sampaguita* leis, which they placed around our necks as they bade us farewell. The goodbyes were doubly poignant because we sensed that we'd never come back again.

As we set sail and the people started fading in the distance, it occurred to me that that moment of rest upon the sands of Suclaran and its magic isles would be indelibly pressed into memory, as places where we'd caught a tantalizing glimpse of paradise, but had to move on. It was sad to have to leave this Eden, from where no one was casting us out.

We sailed north, keeping Guimarás to port, always within sight. A mild December sun emptied its quiver of noonday rays on the white-crested ruffles around us. A brisk northwesterly creased the seas so that we had to tack frequently to make any headway. A strange fondness for these frayed, wind-blown waters came back unbidden, making me feel like some errant mariner rediscovering the joy of roaming, insignificant but free, in the teeming vastness of the sea.

"I must have had seafaring ancestors," I confessed to Lawson. "I can sense it in my bones."

"Me too," he answered, his tow hair blowing in the wind. "Norsemen, probably."

"Barbarians, more likely!"

"No more'n those Pyrenean cave-dwelling ancestors of yours! Talk about primitive!"

"Yeah, but at least they left paintings in their caves. Yours just went around pillaging the countryside."

"Oh yeah? We had great knights and kings. Remember King Arthur?" he argued huffily.

"Yeah, and Ethelred the Unready! What a 'keedle' he must'a been!"

Juan gazed on, bemused by the friendly banter, but I could tell he wasn't quite following the nip and tuck. He just sat there at the tiller, looking serene, thinking placid thoughts, daydreaming a mariner's soulful dreams.

It was late afternoon when San Miguel came into view. The village sat almost at the island's northernmost tip, near the edge of the sea. Even in the waning light of evening, we could already glimmer Panay looming across the strait, scarcely four miles away. The northernmost tip of Guimarás hid Iloilo from view. Home was, literally, right around the corner.

After beaching the *parao* and furling its sail, we struck out along the edge of the seacoast town. People stared at us with the curiosity we had grown used to by now. Stilt houses stood with their feet in the water, like so many stilled sandpipers. Juan's niece lived in one of them.

Our unannounced visit caught them a little by surprise. The young couple and their two young children had just started supper, when we turned up. We were ushered into the rickety bamboo hut, with much shaking of hands, hearty backslapping and kiss-sniffing. I'd forgotten how our Yayas used to kiss us that way, when we were children, touching our cheeks with aspirating noses, as if trying to capture each other's life essence with a flitting sniff.

They insisted that we join them at table. It was a tight squeeze but the food was hearty and the company pleasant. The conversation soon focused on us. In his gruff, clipped way, Juan waxed oddly eloquent, narrating our mountain adventures and magnifying our exploits. He now had us wounding every besieging Japanese soldier during our mountain melee.

The conversation dragged on into the night, fisherman talk mixed with war news, and then just plain catching up on family gossip. After Juan's niece got up from the table to put her brood to bed, Lawson and I left the two fishermen to their tall sea tales, and retired to the open porch.

The gentle swaying of the house with every lapping wave, made us sleepy. Crabs scratched and nibbled at the barnacles that studded the stilts holding up the house.

"It'd be funny if those crabs down there ate through one of the ruddy bamboo posts tonight," said Lawson, chuckling.

"Stilts always remind me of that enraged *carabao* that took off with one of them, once," I said, bemused by the slapstick consequences of the one-buffalo stampede Luis and I had provoked, back in the hills of Igbarás.

"What happened?" asked Lawson.

"This farmer, who lived next door, used to let us ride his *carabao*-drawn sled around the countryside. The *carabao* just plodded on, slow as molasses, so Luis and I would prod its balls, trying to make it go faster."

"I bet he got a jolt outta that!" said Lawson, his interest now piqued.

"Not really. But they must have memories like elephants, those *carabaos*. We were horsing around near it, one afternoon, when its eyes suddenly turned bloodshot. It started tugging at the nipa hut's stilt it was hitched to, until, pretty soon, the whole hut starts swaying and collapses, like in slow motion, right there, in front of our very eyes, spilling the farmer's family all over the grounds!"

"You're putting me on!" exclaimed Lawson, giggling at the imagined scene.

"No, I'm not! Ask Luis when we get back. He'll tell you."

"What happened then?" he pursued. "Did anybody get hurt?"

"No, just a little dazed, I suppose. We didn't hang around to watch the aftereffects. See, this *carabao* came chasing after us, hauling this post behind it. We lit out like bats outta hell, with nary a backward glance!"

"Did they find out you did it?"

"I don't think so. The whole town was abuzz with rumors that some evil spirit must'a sneaked up on the *carabao*!

"Did you see the farmer after that?"

"Sure! He lived right next door. Why, only a few days later, Luis and I borrowed his mare without his permission. We rode it bareback, no reins, no nothing, just a rope tied around its snout. Well, we couldn't control it very well, so we strayed into the farmer's paddy, where he was stooping over, ankle deep in water, planting rice shoots."

"Boy, I bet he was mad!" said Lawson, now up on his elbows, all ears.

"Like a wet hen! He straightened out real quick, unsheathes this huge *binangon* machete and comes charging after us, shouting "*Lintî ang Cachilâ!*" ready to slice our heads off."

"How'd you get outta that scrape?"

"Well this dumb mare didn't wanna stop so we jumped off her. That stopped her, and when she did, we turned her around, jumped right back onto her and took off, quick as greased lightning. And not a second too soon, either. The farmer had almost caught up with us by then!"

"Boy, I can just see Dad reading you the Riot Act when he found out. Did he?"

"Yup. Bad news travels fast in them thar hills. We were grounded for a while, after that. That farmer sure hated our guts!"

"Sounds like you guys had fun up there in Igbarás," he said, a little enviously. I didn't respond. Every time I spoke of Igbarás, Lawson got a little sad. That was about the time he lost his folks.

As we lay there on the bamboo floor, gazing at the stars outside the porch, I reflected on the home stretch, the yearning increasingly magnified by the prism of exile.

"We're getting closer to home," I said. "Probably we should just go back to Iloilo directly."

There was a long pause; Lawson had either drifted into sleep or was taking his time mulling over the proposition.

"You mean walk right back into the lion's den?" he asked, a little incredulously.

"Sure! They certainly wouldn't expect us doing anything like that. The last place they'd come looking for us was home. It's like that trick we pulled on them in the mountain, backing onto our own tracks, going towards them instead of away from them. It worked once, didn't it?"

"You do the unexpected once too often and, pretty soon, it becomes predictable," said Lawson, unconvinced. "It's a little like tempting fate."

It wasn't like him to turn down a daunting scheme, and his reluctance now gave me pause. I had always admired his keen logic and analytical mind. He had something like a sixth sense about some things.

"Besides," he added, "there's Antonio and Maling. That's why we left Suclaran in a bit of a hurry, remember?"

"I guess you're right," I answered peevishly, a little embarrassed by my impatience to return home. "We're so close to Jordan now, it'd be a shame not to stop and see them. Besides, we came to help them rebuild their home." The mere thought that they'd, somehow, run afoul of the Japanese renewed the prickle of guilt.

"I wonder if Uyeki was part of that siege in the cave," I mused out loud.

"Perishing bugger!" whispered Lawson hoarsely. "I'm really beginning to dislike the bleeder."

Even in the dark, I knew that he wasn't amused by his own French, this time. Uyeki had been our nemesis for three years running, and he had almost sprung the trap this time around.

20. JORDAN REVISITED

Sea gulls were crying harshly in the quiet air when we sailed into the bay of Jordan, the next morning. The town looked larger than it had when we first sailed past it on the Sea Hawk, a month earlier. The sunken remains of a wooden launch lay in the shallows near the jetty, a mute reminder of the previous week's air raid on Uyeki's expedition.

"I wonder if that tall guerrilla commander we met under the banyan tree radioed the Americans about the Japanese landing in Guimarás," I said, observing the splintered hull of the sunken launch.

"Looks like it," answered Lawson. "They sure did a proper job on that boat!"

The *paraos* beached along the length of the sandy bay resembled grounded whales, sunbathing on the Sabbath. Fishermen squatted by the fishing nets spread out on the sand, sewing the ragged holes in them, leaving lumpy, graceless knots, as male seamstresses sometimes do.

"Let's go see your priends pirst," suggested Juan after we'd dragged the *parao* onto dry land. "We'll decide what to do apter that. I hope you remember where they live."

Taking our bearings from the marketplace where we had once shopped, we struck out along the familiar back alleys toward the outskirts of town, where Juan lived. I noticed that people were watching us with a mixture of curiosity and apprehension.

"That's the Lazarus look, if I ever saw one," commented Lawson, noticing the cautious reserve in the passersby's sudden turning of heads and suspicious glances. "I don't see any kids following us like they used to, either," he added.

"I hope it's shyness and not unfriendliness," I commented, a little concerned now of having worn out our welcome. It could only mean one thing, and the possibility wasn't a pleasant one.

Juan, who had said little since we landed, spoke up. "You boys worry too much, bepore you have to. These people think you were either killed by the Japs - which now makes you ghosts - or they associate you with Japanese visits. Either way, they're suspicious."

We walked on, troubled now by the old fisherman's sensible revelation. I sensed that we may have worn thin this people's hospitality. It was a little late to undo the trouble we had already visited on this gentle people, but the time to return home was drawing nearer than I thought.

As we left the last huts of town behind us, we peered keenly at the foothills, hoping to see Antonio's two-story house in the distance.

"It's there! It still stands!" Lawson cried out

"Yee ha!" I rejoined, caught up in the excitement, even though I still couldn't see it. Soon, however, the two-story structure loomed in the distance. Caught up in the elation of the moment, Lawson and I started hugging and jumping up and down in circles around the old fisherman. Juan looked on, bemused by our antics, looking a little envious of the youth and exuberance that the young so mindlessly splurge, sometimes.

Lawson and I rushed off toward the house, leaving Juan behind to follow at his own plodding gait. Dashing up the steps to the house's landing, we knocked on the door and called out their names. Malíng opened the door tentatively and, for a split second, just stood there in the doorway, mouth agape, eyes wide with wonder and disbelief.

Recovering from her initial shock, she threw her arms around us, crying: "Oh, thank God you're alive! We thought you were dead!" she cried, tears welling up in her soft brown eyes.

"It's so good to see you again! You look so good! And here we were praying for you and having votive Masses while you go pulling a dead man's stunt on us. You naughty boys," she chided teasingly. "But don't just stand there. Come in. I'm sure you have lots to talk about," she said, ushering us into the house.

Alerted by the commotion, her two older children came rushing into the room and flung themselves at us, squealing in delighted recognition. Malíng stuck her head out of one of the living room windows and called out to her husband, who was working in the backyard:

"Antonio!" she cried out, still breathless with excitement. "Come, hurry! Guess who's back!"

Antonio came galumphing up the back steps, wiping his soiled hands on his work pants. Like Malíng before him, he stopped dead in his tracks, dumbstruck on first seeing us. Recovering from his surprise, he rushed over to embrace us.

"You're alive!" he exclaimed, wide eyed. "I can't believe it!"

"Yup!" I answered casually. "Safe and sound. We made it!"

"But the cave was demolished!" he persisted in his disbelief. "I saw it with my own two eyes! We pigured you must hab put up a good pight, though. We saw a lot of spent cartridges lying about. How could you possibly have survived that disaster?" He paused breathlessly for answers.

"Did you notice that hole in the roof, toward the back of the cave?" I asked, grinning broadly. "We got out through there between blasts. We were really lucky with our timing. A little deaf but unhurt, as you can see."

"Yes, we saw the hole. Por a while there I suspected you might have escaped through it, but then I thought it was too high up in the roop to reach. Besides, we knew it was impossible to survive those hand grenade blasts. We saw all the shrapnel, you see. But we couldn't pind any bloodstains.

229

That puzzled us. And then we couldn't pind your bodies anywhere. So we gave you a proper puneral, just in case."

"Well, we managed to give them the slip," said Lawson, "dog and all! By the way, how did that hound get our drift? We worried about that a lot the last few days."

"Thereby hangs a tale," interjected Malíng. "They threatened some child in town when they landed and porced inpormation out of its mother. They made a beeline por our house apter that. We knew they were coming; we'd been porewarned. So we took opp in the nick of time. They must have discovered that soiled T-shirt of yours," she said, looking at Lawson. "You know, the one that had C.S.A. printed on its back. It looked so poreign they probably knew it had to be yours. By the way, what did those initials stand for?"

"Colegio San Agustín," said Lawson, grinning peevishly. "That's our school."

"We pound it lying on the ground, near the cave," Juan continued. "It was stupid of us to leave it lying around the house. But we had to scram out of here in a big hurry."

There was a bashful knock at the front door. Juan had finally caught up with us. Malíng opened the door and let him in, after I introduced him. Antonio and Malíng were puzzled at first by our far flung acquaintances. We described our escape to Suclaran and explained how Juan had befriended us and sailed us back to Jordan.

"I guess you're lucky. They didn't burn your house down, apter all," commented Juan. "These boys really worried about that all these past pew days. As a matter of pact, that's why they're here now. They insisted on coming to help you rebuild it."

Malíng gave us a warm, motherly smile, her eyes misting over with emotion. "*Ang batáan ko*," she whispered almost inaudibly, bursting with motherly pride; she had just claimed us as her own children. Juan had also fallen silent, touched by the revelation.

"We'd heard someone's house had burned down," said Lawson, trying to break the awkward silence. "We were almost sure it was yours."

"An old abandoned house by the wharp was burned. A machine gun tracer bullet must have set it apire when they sank one of the launches moored on the jetty. That sinking really shook them up. You should have seen them piling aboard the other two remaining launches and skidaddling opp. We thought they were going to sink! That was our chance to let them have it. But cooler heads prevailed," he said, almost apologetically. "We didn't want them coming back and setting Jordan to the torch. So we just let them go."

"Stealth is wealth," commented Lawson. I didn't detect any sarcasm in his voice as he parroted the old guerrilla lesson. He continued: "Someone told us in Suclaran that some Jap had been wounded in the firefight with us. Is that true?"

"Yes!" Antonio answered, intrigued that we'd heard. "Their Lieutenant was hit on the arm by one op your bullets! The same town doctor who treated you for your boar wound was roused out of bed in the middle of the night and porced to tend to his wound. We were really proud of the pight you two put up, up there. Like our Colonel said, you boys did more por the cause in one night than this whole outpit of ours has done since the war started. Wait till the troop hears you're alive!"

"What did this wounded lieutenant look like," I asked, curious now.

"The doctor didn't go into any great detail," said Antonio. "He did comment on his myopia, though. Round, steel-rimmed glasses. Spoke pretty decent Visayâ. That impressed Dr. Manúud."

"Uyeki!" Lawson and I blurted out in unison, looking at each other. "I thought that voice behind the megaphone sounded familiar!" I added.

"What are you boys talking about?" asked Malíng, puzzled by the cryptic interchange.

"This fellow is like our own private Captain Hook," I volunteered in way of explanation. "He's been chasing us for a while now. Thinks Lawson here belongs in concentration camp. I guess being wounded by us isn't going to help things any. It sure isn't going to dampen his enthusiasm for the chase. The beggar might bring a whole Company over, next time."

I paused for a moment before adding what had been in my mind for a while now. "I really think it's time for us to leave Guimarás. We've visited enough excitement on your island already."

A pall seemed to suddenly fall over the reunion. It was Malíng who broke the awkward silence.

"But where could you boys possibly go?" she asked, disappointed by the thought of seeing us leave again when we had just returned, safe and sound.

"Back to Iloilo," I answered firmly. "We've already discussed it. They'll never expect to find us back home. That's the last place they'd come looking for us. Besides, we'll finally get out of your hair, that way."

"Sounds pretty risky to me," said Antonio. "Ip you wait a week or so, the sub could pick you up and take you to Australia. You'd be sape there."

"We've already decided against that," said Lawson, unequivocally. "Our folks are waiting for us in Iloilo. Their fate will be our fate."

"You are right," said Malíng in a resigned tone. "Much as we'd love to have you with us, you belong with your parents. Your mother is probably worried sick about you. How do you plan to get back to Iloilo?"

"I will take them," offered Juan. "I promised them that. It won't take but a couple of hours to get there. But I suggest we set sail tonight, when it gets dark. It'll be saper that way."

Malíng looked heartbroken. She had been looking forward to spoiling us again, as she had during our extended stay with them.

"Very well, then," said Antonio. "You boys are old enough to make your own decisions. God knows you've made a few pateful ones this past week alone. I hope your luck holds out."

I liked the way Antonio had always respected our decisions and given us the benefit of mature judgment.

"You boys run along now," said Malíng. "I'll have to get busy with early dinner."

It turned out to be a memorable short-order farewell feast. The menu included varied western Visayan delicacies like *batchoy* pork soup, *pancit* noodles, and a heaping main dish of delicious *calamares* on a bed of rice.

I couldn't help but reflect that this could be our last square meal in a long spell. The besieged town we were headed for had already been suffering severe food shortages even before we left it, over a month earlier. I almost felt a sense of guilt as I speared the last slice of *kalamansi*-squirted papaya from the desert bowl.

It had turned dark by the time we got up from the table. Malíng had lit the wicks of several small, coconut oil-fueled earthenware lamps strewn around the room. The tiny flames quivered at first as they sputtered to life, and then burned gently, spilling their calm across the darkening room. The time for farewells had come.

"We will miss you two," said Malíng, as she hugged first Lawson and then me. "You boys have stolen into our hearts and plucked at our apppection," she continued softly, drawing our faces down to hers and sniffing our cheeks in the ancient Malayan ritual of fondness. "You must come again someday."

A sudden tightness in the throat threatened to leave me speechless. "Thanks for everything," I managed to say inadequately. "You've gone through a lot of trouble for us. We'll never forget you," I added, giving her a big hug.

"Wish we could thank you properly," said Lawson when his turn came. I knew he was also at the edge of emotion. "We'll come back to see you someday, when this war's over."

"I'm sorry you couldn't stay a while longer," said Antonio, as we started down the steps. "The troop would have enjoyed listening to your adventures. I know the Captain would have pinned some medals on you. He's a stickler por porm. Probably I'll send them on to you by messenger one of these days."

"They'll get a kick out of that back home," I said. "Thanks again for everything," I added, hugging him tightly.

As we waved farewell, I realized that by having risked his family's wellbeing by taking us in, Antonio had given a full measure of kindness and generosity. I knew that gifts like this could never be repaid.

The streets of Jordan were deserted as the three of us headed for the beach. Only the light of the waning moon lit our way to Juan's *parao*. The boat lay on the dark sand, leaning on one of its outriggers, like a sleeping animal with one leg sticking up in the night air.

We pulled the *parao* toward the edge of the sea, until it bobbed gently in the shallows. One by one, we piled into it. Being the last one in, I gave the boat one last shove before clambering aboard, realizing that I was touching Guimarás for the last time. We had blundered from nightmare to fairytale in that enchanted isle, a land of waking dreams where beauty and death had touched hands and then parted, to grant us the grace of another day.

The trip across the glassy strait was slow and uneventful. Nothing moved in the murky blackness except the speck of winged flotsam bearing an old fisherman and two homesick boys across the narrow strait. There were no lights anywhere in sight in that midnight hour. Juan was actually steering by the feel of the small wind on his face.

Soon, the outline of Iloilo loomed up ahead, dull against the night sky. As we approached the land mass of Panay, the Iloilo River's mouth yawned in welcome. Juan steered clear of the river, pointing the *parao* toward the southern edge of town. Shortly after, the *parao's* keel scraped the sand, almost at the same spot where we had sailed off on the Sea Hawk, in brazen challenge of the military order. The nuns' convent brooded above us, deep in sleep. Soon, they'd be singing their Matins to the new day.

"Well, this is it," said Juan after all three of us had jumped off the boat onto the beach. "I guess this is goodbye."

He patted us on the shoulder affectionately, slightly embarrassed by the thought of men hugging in farewell. In his own awkward way, the old fisherman struggled with the bitter sweetness of parting, and its intimations of endings and of death.

"I guess you boys know your way home from here," he said in his gravelly voice, turning as if to leave.

I reached over and embraced him, despite his embarrassment at such shows of affection. "Thanks for everything, Juan. You were kind to us and helped us in our hour of need, even at great risk. I'll never forget you. *Vaya con Dios, mi amigo.*"

Lawson shook the old fisherman's hand. "That was awful nice of you," he said limply, "doing all this for us. *Salamat gid* and Godspeed, old friend."

We stood there on the beach, waving at the old fisherman until his sailboat disappeared in the stillness of the December night. I sensed that something good and noble had silently sailed in and out of our lives, enriching them with the brief encounter. Juan had been for us a pure blessing.

21. HOME FROM THE HILL

The town was folded in darkness as we wove our way up Calle Ortiz, heading for the town square. Atayde's mongrel barked at us several times, and then crawled back despondently into its doghouse. The bell in the church's clock tower chimed twice, its deep notes bouncing about the buildings around Plaza Libertad. The old Masonic Temple appeared unguarded in the pre-dawn hour, as we snuck past its massive, brass-studded front door. Turning the corner of Calle Real, we dashed the short remaining distance for home.

The wrought iron gate was padlocked tight. Skipping around to the back of the house, we scaled the high, spear-tipped grille fence and dropped into the compound, near the water well. Startled, Eusebio's new gamecock cackled territorial assertions before settling back to its rooster dreams.

Lobo dozed fitfully at the foot of the stairway. Raising a lazy eyeball in the direction of the startled rooster, the German shepherd let out an unconvincing woof, more in stupor than in challenge. Suddenly recognizing us, the dog ran over to greet us in a tail-wagged weave. He jumped on us, paws playfully clawing at our chests, moaning pleasurably when rubbed behind the ears. The brief, uncomplicated greeting heralded the long-awaited welcome of homecoming.

Trying not to awaken the household, we tiptoed gingerly up the main stairway, avoiding the rungs we knew squeaked. We groped our way around the large dining room table, and made for our bedroom, just across from the upstairs patio. Luis was sound asleep in his bed, but the rustling of our bed sheets aroused him.

"Who's there?" he said with a start, sitting bolt upright in his bed and reaching for the baseball bat resting by his headboard.

"Hi, kid," I spoke in hushes. "Take it easy. It's just us, back from the dead."

"What? Who died?" he asked. "Oh, hi guys," he said, groping out of a dreamy fogbank. "How'd it go? How'd you get here?"

"Just sailed back from Guimarás. Is everything O.K. at home?"

"Uyeki's been looking for you two guys," he answered, wide awake now. "He's been giving Dad a hard time. They hauled him off to Kempitai Headquarters twice already, about a week ago. They didn't beat him up or anything, but they sure grilled him; gave him the once over. They kept him up all night. Mom was pretty shook up."

"How's Dad taking it?" asked Lawson. "Is he mad at us?"

"Certainly not!" he answered huffily. "He says you guys did the right thing. Uyeki's not buying any of that adoption story, though. 'Sham!' Dad said he kept shouting every time he brought it up. You know how testy the bastard gets. Anyway, they threatened to come and turn the house upside down. Must'a thought you two were hiding out in here, somewhere."

"How'd they find out we were in Guimarás?" I asked, perplexed. "They came looking for us there, you know."

"I knew it!" he said worriedly. "Well, let me tell you what happened. They came in here one afternoon, lined up the help in the patio downstairs, and started grilling them, one by one. The servants knew about Guimarás, of course. We'd told them, you see. Nobody cracked at first. Then Uyeki grabbed the cook's youngest kid by the scruff of the neck and jerked him around pretty good, until the kid started shrieking like a stuck pig. Well, that was more'n his mother could handle, so she spilled the beans."

"What happened then?" asked Lawson, now on pins and needles.

"They just stormed out'a here, mad as wet hens. Shoved people around as they left, casting all sorts of threats," said Luis.

"What kind of threats?" I pursued.

"Something about hauling the whole lot of us to jail if they ever found you two. He looked like he meant it, too." Luis paused for a second and then, changing the subject, he added: "Boy, it's sure good to see you guys back home again. It's been kind'a spooky around here without you two. You'll have to keep a real low profile for a while, though. You must be on the top of Uyeki's black list. You're lucky he didn't find you!"

"Well, he sure tried," I answered. "But we managed to keep one step ahead of him. He brought a hound along with him. Almost sniffed us out. That was one close call."

"You should'a seen the firefight we got into with them in this cave up in the hills. It made Tim McCoy's shoot-em-up's at the Bar X Ranch look like piddle kid stuff!" said Lawson, stumbling over himself with excitement. "And then the perishing buggers started lobbing ruddy hand grenades at us! They like'a busted our eardrums. My ears rang for several days after that. I'm still a little deaf."

"Hot damn!" Luis kept interjecting throughout the story. He wanted to know every detail of our month's absence. Lawson and I were, of course, happy to oblige. Like relay runners in a track race, we took turns recounting the odyssey in a low monotone that droned on until dawn, interrupted only by Luis' occasional expressions of disbelief and excitement.

As I lay there in the dark, listening to Lawson describe our brush with the Japanese, my mind turned each event, savoring its memory with the amazement of danger, challenged and overcome. In this state of detached consciousness, the realization that we were the main characters in the saga came with the small touch of pride.

The war stories dragged on until the first rays of the sun came streaming over the roof of the patio outside. We were enveloped in a cloud of laughter, recounting Lawson's dancing exploits in Suclaran, when Mom, awakened by the guffaws, suddenly walked into the room.

Leaping up from bed, we hugged in inarticulate greeting, choked by the emotion of the long-awaited encounter. Tears of joy streamed down my face, as they had many years earlier, after a summer's absence in Pilar.

"Thank God you're back!" Mom kept repeating, caressing our faces time and again, as if disbelieving her sense of sight. "I was sure my little Virgin of Roncesvalles would keep you safe and bring you back unharmed!"

Mom had always been a deeply religious woman. I was convinced that her relentless prayers eventually beat her saints into relieved submission, that her blind faith and almost childish trust in them finally shamed them into grudging intervention.

"This is the best Christmas gift you could have given me," she said, feasting her eyes on her two lost children. We had suspected the season was close at hand but didn't realize it was already Christmas Eve.

"That was great timing, wasn't it," said Lawson. "Now we can celebrate it properly, like Christmas and the Three Kings, all rolled into one!"

"Come, we must wake the others," Mom said, holding back her thousand unasked questions so the others could share in the first telling. That was just like her, too, Mom, the soul of generosity. She hadn't changed a bit. We all trundled over to Mom and Dad's bedroom, waking everyone up as we went.

Having heard the excitement, Dad had already finished dressing, half suspecting the cause of the commotion.

"*Gure maita mutiko*," he whispered as we embraced. Only the hoarseness in his voice betrayed his emotion. 'My dear child,' he had said in Basque. his native and ancient tongue. "It is good to see you again," he added expansively. "I am proud of you."

It was a powerful moment of rare visitation, when two generations touched intimately for a flitting instant of naked honesty, and then let go, a little embarrassed by the display of raw feeling. It was good that the room was still in semi darkness; I would not have understood the mistiness in his eyes. I only suspected that he was gripped by the same emotion as I.

One by one, the others came stumbling into the master bedroom, rubbing sleep from their eyes, disbelieving what they were seeing. Consolación, the Yaya, pulled our heads down to her five-foot height, and proceeded to sniff our cheeks in hearty welcome.

"*Ay abaw, que guapos!*" she exclaimed, commenting on our physical appearance, enhanced now by the deep suntan and added weight we'd put on since they last saw us.

The questions started sedately enough at first but soon came in fast flurries, stumbling over unfinished responses; as if afraid the particulars would dull, if left too long unquestioned. After the night's dry run with Luis, we fielded their questions with increasing embellishment, carefully avoiding mention of the dicier points, like the shootout at the cave. There was no point in worrying Mom. We elaborated on Guimarás instead, describing our wanderings through its forested mountains, the kindness of its gentle, hospitable people, and the exotic foods with which they regaled us during our month of absence.

After the story telling, Mom swung into action. She now had a more special Christmas Eve dinner to plan for, our return calling for a special celebration. There were few occasions when Christmas would again coincide with the homecoming of two prodigal children. Knowing how much we loved the dish, she asked Angel to prepare 'Cuban Rice' for dinner.

He looked at her with puzzled expression. "But we need eggs for that, *Señora*. You know we can't get them any more."

"I'll take care of that," she answered with conviction. Summoning the old lady with whom she had bartered all her silverware and good china during the preceding months, Mom was now ready to pull off one last deal.

"How much for a dozen eggs?" she asked the wizened old lady when she turned up, half an hour later.

Smiling crookedly, the old woman looked down at Mom's hands. With a straight face, she answered:

"Your solitaire."

Mom was taken aback by the outrageous proposition. She had bartered her wedding ring away months earlier but had, somehow, managed to hang on to her diamond engagement ring. It was her last remaining precious possession, and she'd been saving it for one last emergency. She must have concluded that the price and timing were right because, upon brief reflection, she pulled the ring off her finger and closed the lopsided deal.

When Angel cracked the eggs later that evening, he was aghast to discover that every single one of them was rotten.

Mom tried to make light of the pathetic episode. "This would have made a great O'Henry story," she quipped, like a good sport. But the poignant incident touched us all with a sense of loss. Its pathos hung like a pall over what would have been a memorable homecoming celebration. Instead, we had Mongo beans and *tancong* greens for supper that evening.

"We must find a hiding place for you two boys," Dad said during dinner. "Uyeki could pay us a surprise visit any time." After a short pause, he added: "You can't hide upstairs. It wouldn't be safe with all these bombings. We've been spending more and more time downstairs, by the shelter. But that wouldn't do for you two. It's within view of the main gate and you'd be spotted instantly."

"How about the basement?" I suggested. "We can spend our days there, reading or playing chess, or something else. We could sneak behind the big water cistern under the main stairway, during the raids. It's a great hiding place and as good a shelter as the new one."

Having agreed on the scheme, Lawson and I went into seclusion. In case Uyeki dropped by, the warning signal would be two honks from the truck's goose horn. Much to

245

Juan Sumalakay's distress, he had to unscrew it from the old Ford and bolt it onto the shelter's entrance, for easy access.

Lawson and I seldom saw the light of day for days on end in that huge basement. We lost our tan in no time and quickly got used to the old, humdrum fare of corn meal and Mongo soup. Luis and the Arana brothers spent most of their time with us in the basement. We played basketball with a tennis ball, shooting it through a small wire hoop nailed to the back of a door.

When we tired of basketball, we boxed, using the pair of gloves Dad had ordered for us from Sears, years earlier. They barely fit now, but since we all had to share them, the sweat-sodden leather yielded enough to fit most any size fist now. Luis had grown visibly during our absence. Having lost my old reach advantage, I could no longer slip him my old punches; he merely kept me at bay with his long gangly arms. I realized that our boxing days were numbered.

Sometimes, we'd play Naval Conquest, a table game where toy lead warships were moved around on a crosshatched board of ocean, using dice to determine the number of moves. The object of the game was to sink the enemy's fleet or capture his home base. My favorite tactic was to lie in ambush behind a group of smallish islands in the middle of the board, which afforded submarines and destroyers a sporting chance against more powerful Men-of-War. Besides, the islets reminded me of Nalunga and Nadulao.

Chess was the pastime of last resort. Luis had gotten even better at it during our absence. Ybiernas, the town's Mayor and undisputed chess champion, occasionally challenged Luis to a game, splitting Check Mates with him. So our chess games with Luis turned into lopsided routs. Lawson, who was big on fairplay, didn't think the matches were being fought on a level playing field and ignored Luis' persistent challenges.

Outside, the war ground on relentlessly. Bombings were redoubled, in early 1945. Flying in around mid morning, American fighter-bombers would drop their bomb load on ships anchored in the river nearby and leave, after the ritual strafing passes. During the bombings, Lawson and I hid behind the water cistern under the main stairway. The dark, dank air there only added to the sinister atmosphere.

"The water in this tank behind us would probably save us even from a direct hit," commented Lawson one day, "We'd have a helluva time swimming out from under the deluge, though. Did you ever think of that?" We stopped ducking there for shelter after that. We simply continued reading or playing, when the sirens sounded. Since we were by ourselves most of the time, nobody knew the difference.

Our seclusion seemed to drag on interminably. We sorely missed the freedom of Guimarás and slowly slipped into a kind of dream world, where freedom became dimly apprehended and only viscerally understood. We begged Dad to let us spend our seclusion upstairs, where we could at least see the sun from the porch. It took some convincing but he finally relented.

"We must find a good hiding place for you on the second floor," he said, torn between the equally risky hazards of flying shrapnel and a surprise visit from Uyeki.

"I know a great hiding place," I said, pressing our advantage. "How about the attic? They'd never find us there!"

"It's not easy to get to quickly enough," Dad commented, pursing his lips, in deep thought.

"It's a cinch!" I said with conviction. "You know that small trap door above the water filter in the pantry? I used to lift Iru up through it to go sic those rats we used to have up there. Remember?"

"Yes, I remember," he answered. "That's probably as good a hiding place as any. Probably even better than the basement."

It was settled, then. Lawson and I moved from the basement to the upstairs quarters, on condition that we rush down to the shelter at the first hint of an air raid. The change did wonders for our morale. The warm, cleansing touch of sunshine on our faces, alone, was invigorating.

Despite the admonition of not straying far from the attic trapdoor, we started wandering over to the patio, more and more often. Sometimes, we'd even clamber up the narrow iron ladder to the roof. There, we'd lie on the warm corrugations of the many-gabled roof and dream of the things we'd do when the war ended. We'd lie there for hours on end, hands clasped behind our heads, gazing up at the sky above, vacant save for the occasional seagull, crying harshly in the still air.

"I wonder what those heathery moors in the Highlands really look like," Lawson mused, his visions taking him far beyond the wan Philippine sky above.

"A tumble in the heather with a bonnie lassie," he added, giggling. "Mr. McPherson, that was his name! Tom McPherson! He liked to sing bawdy songs when he got tipsy at home. I remember this ditty of his that went 'Oh, tickle me under the kiltie, and under the kiltie and you know where..'" Lawson howled with laughter, the reminiscence washing over him with waves of cleansing mirth.

"Jesus Jimenez would love that," I said, imagining his keen brown eyes crinkling up at the risqué ballad. "He'd probably come up with a few raunchy lyrics of his own."

"I wonder what the delinquent is up to these days," Lawson harrumphed.

Ever since they were kids, there had always been a latent rivalry between Lawson and Jesus Jimenez. Their different characters and cultural backgrounds may have had something to do with it; one with the splattered and outrageous wit of a Mediterranean, the other with the sober reticence of a Saxon. As I look back on it now, I always seemed to be playing the role of the peacemaker between them.

The sound of the goose horn suddenly broke through our consciousness, its flatulent notes striking unpremeditated terror in us.

"Bloody hell!" cried Lawson, raising himself on his elbows. "They're here!" he exclaimed, eyes bugging out in near panic.

It only took a second to get over our initial shock. Diving for the roof ladder, we skipped down its rungs, three at a time, dropping onto the patio floor and making a hasty retreat for the pantry. As we crouched past the main stairway's landing, we heard harsh commands above the din of a barking dog, downstairs.

Bounding up a chair purposely left by the water filter, we clambered up to the narrow crawl space between the wall-to-wall cupboards and the ceiling. Pushing open the small trapdoor above our heads, we squirmed up into the darkness of the attic and closed the trapdoor behind us.

We crouched in the dark, hearts pounding audibly against our throats. A dank odor of old wood and disturbed dust filled our nostrils, ancient cobwebs feebly tugging at our eyelids. No one had been up there since the house was built, a century earlier; no one, that is, except Iru and the rats.

"I wonder if Iru got all those rats up here," Lawson whispered.

"Doesn't much matter now," I answered in hushes. "We won't be up here long enough to find out, one way or the other."

"Listen!" he murmured with sudden urgency. "They're right below us now!"

A dog was barking almost directly under the trapdoor. It was the same unforgettable yelp we'd heard outside the cave in Guimarás. The manic, deep-throated baying aroused memories of livid terror, as only some sounds can.

A clatter of boots followed, rushing first toward the kitchen and the help's quarters, and then back again to the dining room. There must have been half a dozen troops looking for us.

The blood-curdling yelps increased in intensity, sounding, now, as if the bloodhound were barking directly at the trap door beneath us. There was an increased babble of staccato commands in the pantry. We froze, holding our breath as if mimicked death could, somehow, forestall the real thing. In his panic, Lawson was unconsciously gripping my arm in a painful vice.

"This is it!" he whispered almost inaudibly.

The barking suddenly redoubled under us. There was a rumble of frantic snarling and growling, accompanied by anguished yelps and smothered howls, followed, finally, by sounds of gnashing teeth. It almost sounded like a dogfight.

"Lobo!" I whispered. The pent-up terror suddenly drained from me, leaving me limp with relief. Lobo was challenging the interloper of his domain, distracting the hound from its deadly and nearly-accomplished task. Several shouted commands rose above the din; someone was trying to separate the fighting dogs. The ferocious howling persisted, unabated.

Suddenly, a shot rang out in the afternoon. There was a pained yelp and then, just as suddenly as it had started, the snarling ceased. For a brief moment, there was utter silence. Then a command was given, followed by the sound of scraping boots, shuffling out of the pantry below and toward the hall. The clatter of boots receded down the stairs, and then they were gone.

Lawson and I remained motionless a while longer. I then cracked the trap door open, just enough to see the pantry below us. Lobo's limp body lay motionless, curled up at the foot of the water filter, as if asleep. I was hoping, against all hope, that my suspicions were unfounded and that he'd still be alive. But there were no sounds of life, only a small pool of blood spreading under his head.

"I can't believe it!" said Lawson, leaning over my shoulder to gaze on the scene below. "The perishing bugger's done it again!"

I was too stunned to answer. I had felt the same pain and outrage when Iru died, but the sense of déjà-vu offered little comfort and even fewer explanations to malevolence.

The rest of the family came rushing into the pantry, terrified by the sound of the shot. Expecting the worst, they were relieved to see us both unscathed. Lawson and I climbed down from the attic. We all stood silently around the lifeless form of Lobo, moved by the animal's noble selflessness.

"It was Uyeki, wasn't it?" I asked no one in particular, knowing the answer before it was given.

"Yes," said Luis. "He was laughing when he left."

22. HOLOCAUST

"Do you suppose they're bombs?" asked Lawson warily.

We'd been lying on the roof, whiling away the hours, when the lone P-38 startled us with its roar. We were amazed at how suddenly it had materialized, flying so low and fast that it was, all of a sudden, zooming away into the harmless sky before we'd even heard it.

Trailing behind it, a cloud of fluttering objects glinted in the sun on their lazy descent to earth. The last time we'd seen anything like it, the objects had turned out to be a string of bombs. But that was a distant day and a different circumstance, when the flight of B-17s had vomited their entrails on the Jaro airfield, in the outskirts of town. This one was a lone fighter whose solitary noonday visit was, in itself, an oddity.

The shimmering cloud took forever to descend. It had to be something light and harmless, I thought.

"They're leaflets!" I said finally, convinced they could hardly be anything else. We waited for one of them to waft on down to the roof. When one finally did, I snatched it before the wind could blow it out of reach.

The invasion had taken place that morning, the message proclaimed, somewhere beyond Otón, several miles west of town. Iloilo, the note confidently stated, would be liberated soon. Civilians were asked to keep under cover until the city was secured.

"They've landed on Panay!" I shouted out in unrepressed joy. "If you believe in miracles, this is it!"

"Yee ha!" echoed Lawson, trying to read over my shoulder. "Jolly good show, Yanks!"

Lawson and I started dancing a crazy jig along the broad gutter joining two of the roof's many gables. We had waited more than three years for this moment. Now, at last, the little piece of paper in my hand announced the glad tidings. Liberation was at hand.

As we were thus engaged, the P-38 came into view, once again, this time headed straight at us. It was now flying at rooftop level, as if ascertaining where the leaflets had fallen. We waved the piece of paper frantically at it as it approached, the awesome roar of its twin Allison engines engulfing us in its downwash.

We could have reached out and touched its wings as it whooshed past, it flew so close. The pilot's face was clearly visible behind the canopy of the slick, silver warplane; he was waving at us! And then, as if in one last gesture of recognition, he dipped the plane's wings slowly, to and fro, like a dog wagging its tail in friendly gesture.

"Gorblime! Didj'a see that!" cried Lawson in disbelief. "He waved back at us! And he was smiling when he did it, too!" he added breathlessly.

"And then he rolled the plane, as if to say 'hi'!" I rejoined, just as ecstatically.

I stood there, speechless, gripped by an ineffable joy. Here was my very favorite airplane acknowledging my admiration for it! Some moments are frozen in time; for me, that was one of them. I could not believe our immense good fortune of having tarried on the roof, instead of flying down the stairs to the shelter, at the first hint of the airplane's approach.

"I wish I could'a taken a picture of that," I said wistfully. "Didj'a notice the tiny airfoils on the fuselage? Must be a new design. And those air intakes looked larger than in my model." I was mentally comparing subtle design differences between this plane and the earlier vintage Lightning, that I knew so well from pre-war magazines.

We rushed downstairs to share the news of the landing with the rest of the family. They were already in a festive mood, having themselves retrieved several leaflets bearing the good news. Everyone was kissing and hugging, congratulating each other for having endured, thus far. The war was not yet over but the end was near. Everyone had been convinced we'd been bypassed. There was little reason for the Americans to double back and liberate our southern island, when their main thrust lay to the north.

"It's an unmitigated miracle!" remarked Mom. "I knew St. Joseph would come through!" she added, as if in a mystic trance. It was the 19th of March, the Saint's day. There was little doubt in her mind that he had planned the landing himself.

"Yes," hedged Mrs. Arana, "but won't the Japanese dig in and take us out with them?"

Though untimely, the dour remark was not wholly unfounded. We didn't know it then but the entire Spanish colony in Manila had perished, less than a month earlier, along with a hundred thousand other civilians, when the Japanese Army decided to dig in and engage the advancing Americans in bloody, house-to-house combat.

"A cornered enemy is doubly dangerous," Dad reminded the revelers, "particularly if they're Japanese. These people don't give up easily." His comment on the lingering danger dampened the group's premature celebration.

He gave instructions to have the main, wrought iron gate padlocked, ordering everyone to move mattresses and bare essentials down to the basement. We were to huddle there and keep out of sight until the emergency subsided.

The younger crowd started getting restive by mid afternoon. With the excuse of retrieving some reading material, Pedro Mari Arana and I snuck upstairs to have a peek at the outside world. Through the shutter slats in the living room windows, we observed a squad of Japanese engineers digging square, foot-deep holes on the street below us. Right behind them, another squad deposited round, metallic objects inside each gaping hole, gingerly covering it all up with dirt.

"Land mines!" I whispered. The chevron-patterned spacing between holes ensured that no vehicle could proceed without running over one of them.

"I wonder if we can detonate those things with our slingshots from up here," whispered Pedro Mari. Noticing my quizzical look, he quickly added: "When they're gone, of course."

"Guess where the shrapnel's gonna fly up to when you're through doing that, you nutmeg!" I answered smugly. "We'd better hustle on back before they miss us."

We spent a fitful night, hardly sleeping for all the shooting in the outskirts of town. Encouraged by the American landing, the guerrillas had turned frisky and were lighting up the night sky with a hemorrhage of tracer bullets. Occasionally, we'd hear the plinking sound of spent bullets landing harmlessly on our roof.

The women prayed endless strings of rosaries that night, while Dad and Mr. Arana kept staggered watches during the long vigil. Amused by the hysterical drama building up around us, Lawson and I whiled the sleepless hours giggling at each other's sonorous reports. Luis and the Aranas joined in the contest until, pretty soon, the tooting symphony drowned out both the prayers around us and the distant sounds of battle, raging in the outskirts. The women's disgruntled attempts at retrieving the high pious ground only redoubled the pitch of flatulence.

We soon tired of the game and turned our attention on Floríng, the Arana's young maid, who was undressing in the semidarkness. We strained mightily to glimpse her terse young form against the dim light of a flickering lamp, until we finally fell asleep, lulled by the background symphony of whining bullets and the bass-drum thump of distant mortars.

Loud explosions, these ones nearby, woke us up at dawn. We were perplexed, at first, because there was no sound of airplanes or warning whistle of incoming shells. The thunderous blasts shook the house to its foundations. Large rocks came crashing down on the roof after each explosion, some of them landing in the downstairs patio, where they shattered on impact, littering the grounds with debris. The detonations came at irregular intervals, and persisted throughout the morning.

Picking up one of the stones, Dad looked at it quizzically and then brought it up to his nose, to smell it.

"Dynamite!" he declared, a note of concern in his voice. "They're blowing up the town themselves!"

"How do you know? Why would they do anything like that?" asked Mrs. Arana, eyes distended in terror.

"These stones can only come from concrete buildings," Dad answered calmly. "Only the Japanese occupied them. Maybe it's their way of quickly burying the evidence. Or maybe it's just scorched earth tactics, all over again. Hard to say."

It was noon when the first hint of smoke drifted down to the basement, where we huddled. The acrid smell of burning wood soon pervaded the quarters. The patch of sky visible above the patio outside was now thick with smoke, the sun eclipsed by its ruddy pall. The dark, smudged air was thick with specks of flying ash, whirling heavenward as if from a burnt offering. The city was on fire. It was only a matter of time before our house would feed the holocaust.

I followed Dad out of the basement, to get a breath of fresh air. We were standing by the main, wrought iron gate, wrapped in the gathering dark of noon, when, suddenly, two Japanese soldiers, one of them lugging a jerry can, loomed out of the smoke, only a few feet away from us. We froze. It was too late to duck out of sight; they had already seen us.

Stopping in front of us, they demanded, through grunts and gestures, to be let in. Our house was, obviously, their next target. Dad, who was blocking the entrance, simply ignored them, pretending he didn't understand the command. The Corporal un-shouldered his bayonet-affixed rifle and pointed it at Dad's belly, repeating the order. Dad didn't budge; he just stood there, staring at the soldier.

And then, Dad did an odd thing. Waving his hand at them to go on, he said, in a deep, commanding voice: "*Sigue na!*" motioning them to be on their way.

The unexpected reaction took the soldiers aback, but only momentarily. Recovering from their initial surprise, the infuriated Corporal began thrusting his bayonet repeatedly in Dad's direction.

"Ha-yah!" he shrieked every time he lunged as far forward as the wrought iron gate allowed, stopping only an inch short of Dad's belly. I looked on in terror.

With characteristic sang-froid, Dad stood his ground, unflinching, calling the soldier's bluff. Eyes narrowed in defiance, Dad continued to motion them away with impatient gestures, as if irritated by their insolence.

The unnerved soldiers blinked at the unexpected resistance. The private, who was lugging the jerry can, appeared more confused than his Corporal. He finally tugged at his partner's shirtsleeve, muttering something that sounded vaguely conciliatory.

Still grunting his displeasure, the Corporal made one last feigned thrust at Dad and disengaged. In blanched disbelief, I watched the two soldiers slink back into the smoke-choked street, looking back at us sheepishly, as if hoping for meeker prey elsewhere. Dad just stood there, riveting them with unblinking stare.

It had been a gallant, foolhardy gesture; he had saved his home but almost lost his life trying. I had the unreal feeling of having just witnessed the reenactment of an old bedtime story about burnt ships and sword-furrowed sands. Overcome with pride and relief, I sidled up to him and wrapped my arms around his waist, resting my head on his arm.

"*De tal astilla, tal palo*," I whispered, purposely reversing the proverb. It was a son's rejoicing at his worthy stock, a branch proud of its noble trunk.

Putting his arm around my shoulder, he said: "Come, we must leave this exposed entrance. That was too close for comfort."

Before turning to the safety of the basement, we caught a glimpse of the two soldiers as they approached the house diagonally across the street from ours. After splashing gasoline on the front door and sides of the wooden structure, the Corporal struck a match and tossed it at the dripping door. It caught fire with a loud, whooshing sound. The whole street side of the house lit up like a tinder box, flames licking skyward with the ominous crackle of dying wood.

The two arsonists stood in front of the roaring fire, dancing a macabre jig in celebration of their handiwork. They then literally hot-footed it across the street to the other house on the opposite corner of the street intersection, this one directly south of us. There, they repeated their ghoulish ritual, setting the second building on fire.

Flames from the two separate fires soon coalesced, feeding upon each other's maelstrom. A small whirlwind developed at the intersection, first raising arabesques of dust and then gradually growing in intensity until the surrounding air, quivering with heat, was sucked violently into the raging vortex. The roar of the holocaust soon drowned even the intermittent thumps of dynamite blasts, which had persisted throughout the morning.

We ducked behind the massive stone walls of our house's ground floor. The heat, like a furnace blast on our faces, made breathing difficult. Dad's brow, orange with the reflection of the flames, was furrowed with concern. I could almost see his thoughts churning, the frown betraying the struggle between few and equally dangerous options. The safety of not a few lives had been entrusted to his care; a wrong turn or false start now could easily doom us all.

Suddenly, we heard the shouts of one of the house servants, alerting us that the canvas awnings on the upstairs windows were starting to catch fire. The house, like its two neighbors, was in imminent danger of going up in flames.

Dad swung into action. After ordering several men to douse the awnings, he sent one of the house servants to scout the neighborhood for Japanese soldiers. Informed, shortly after, that the coast was clear, he ordered all women and children to vacate the premises and seek refuge in the parish church on Plaza Libertad, only a block away from home. A growing number of terrified citizens had already sought refuge there, when the dynamiting had started earlier that morning. Dad asked all able-bodied men to remain behind and help him save the house.

He stood by the main gate, watching the frightened group of women and children walk out, one by one, into the inferno of the street. He had the grim look of a shepherd watching his flock leave the threatened pen in search for uncertain haven. As Lawson and I stepped out of the gate with the rest of the evacuees, Dad held us back.

"You two boys stay and help fight the fire," he said.

My heart simply leapt for joy. It was as if he'd uttered a magic phrase in some secret rite of initiation into manhood. A message, silently signaled, had been joyfully acknowledged, a threshold proudly crossed. I was a month into my fifteenth year, barely over the cusp of boyhood, anxious to enter manhood with all its bright promises and dark urgencies.

The men who had escorted the women and children to the church returned to join the bucket brigade, already in full swing. Starting from the spigot on the water cistern under the main staircase, a line of sloshing buckets snaked its way to the upstairs patio, and then up the narrow iron ladder to the hot tin roof. There, men leaned precariously over the edge to douse the burning awnings and cool down the wooden sides of the building's second floor.

I slowly wormed my way to the end of the bucket brigade, positioning myself near the gutter on the house's eastern exposure. The searing heat had already blistered most of the paint off. Gorged with latent heat and on the verge of flashpoint, the underlying wood panels were starting to smoke. A sizzling sound, not unlike a sigh of relief, rose from the wooden sidings under me, every time I splashed a bucket of water down the smoldering sides of the house.

From the roof I knew so well, I looked around and saw a city lost in wandering smoke. Cones of flame crowned the nearby fires, dancing among the spark-shot clouds of black smoke billowing from the windows that had started falling in, one by one. The fire was so close by that I could almost reach out and touch the flames. Stung by flying cinders, my ruddy cheeks felt like a bad sunburn. Breathing and seeing had become painful chores. It was like taking in molten lungfulls of acrid air, eyes teary with smoke and cinders.

We had not seen any soldiers on the street below, but we knew, from the lingering dynamite blasts, that the Japanese were still around. Large chunks of stone crashed all around us with clanking thumps, after each detonation. We had stopped covering our heads with our hands, or even ducking instinctively after each blast. It was getting increasingly difficult to move around the debris-littered roof.

Even after an hour of dousing, the corrugated tin roof felt like a lit stove under our feet. But though still raging, the neighboring fires had started to die down perceptively, their flames burning with diminished fury, as if sensing that they were running out of combustibles. I sensed that we had, somehow, beaten the odds against the fire.

23. THE FINAL AGONY

I had just finished emptying a pail of water over the side of the house when a movement on the street below caught my attention. There, less than fifty yards away, a platoon of Japanese soldiers came marching up the road, in smart formation. They were headed west on Calle Real, probably on their way out to the front.

There was no point in ducking out of sight; they had already seen us. Leading the troop was a moon-faced, bespectacled officer, strutting with a vaguely familiar swagger. Our gazes met in a fleeting instant of surprised and mutual recognition.

Uyeki!

I just stood there, frozen in place at the edge of the roof, gripped by a sudden fit of terror. Raising a hand, Uyeki motioned the platoon to a halt. He then pointed a finger at me and belted out a command in Japanese.

As I stood there, exchanging stares with my nemesis, I was suddenly overcome by the same insane urge that had once evoked responses like guffaws at funerals and passing wind in holy places. With studied deliberation, I slowly raised my right hand on high, curled all my fingers shut save the middle one, and shot Uyeki one magnificent bird.

Even from my height, I could see him blink, as the insulting barb sank in. He fumbled for his sidearm, shuddering with fury. Meanwhile, the fifteen soldiers who had been watching me, had un-shouldered their rifles and were ramming a cartridge into their chambers, in ominous bolt action unison.

"Duck! They've spotted us!" I shouted to the others on the roof near me.

With blinding speed, I dove out of the troops' line of fire. I barely hit the roof when the volley rang out, a single deadly report in the smoke-choked afternoon. Pressing my face against the hot tin roof, I felt the thud of fifteen bullets ripping into the gutter where I had stood, only a second earlier. With ghoulish clairvoyance, I suddenly understood the terror of standing in front of a firing squad. My whole short life fleeted past my eyes. I could not believe that I had almost exchanged it for one insane gesture.

"God, please let this guy disappear!" I prayed in fervent supplication, my insides about as petrified as the jagged rock that was digging into my cheek.

I could now hear Uyeki shouting urgent commands at his troops. I knew he'd have trouble forcing the padlocked wrought iron door, or breaching the building's four foot thick walls. But there were easier ways of broaching the compound if the resourceful oriental set his mind to it, and wasn't too pressed for time.

A shadow suddenly streaked across the roof, blocking the hazy sunlight for a fleeting instant. Looking up, I saw an Air Cobra zooming past, almost at rooftop level, its humming roar trailing behind it. It had materialized out of thin air, as if in answer to my prayer. The encircled white stars blazoned on its wings and sides made my heart literally leap for joy inside me.

Looking East, I saw three more slick P-39s trailing the first one, in quick succession. They were lining up along General Hughes Avenue, aluminum skins glistening dully in the smoky twilight of noon. One after another they came, flames spouting ruddily along their wings' leading edges, as they raked Uyeki's distracted platoon.

Crawling back to the roof's edge to observe the drama below, I watched the troops running amok, dispersing helter-skelter, ducking in and out of portals, as they fled toward the center of town. Uyeki was nowhere in sight; he had vanished in thin air, along with his troops.

Only the occasional sound of collapsing beams in the two burning buildings next door broke the eerie silence. The terror was spent, the peril subsided. One by one, the bucket brigade climbed up to the roof and sat down on the soaking tin sheets, for an exhausted respite.

Dad looked at the motley, soot-stained group resting at his feet. "Nice work, fellows!" he said, in his deep, sonorous voice. He was always one to recognize merit and hard work, wherever he saw it. "I'd like to commend you for your courage and great effort. You've saved the house!"

Spoken like a true General, I thought to myself. I couldn't help but think that he would have made a good one.

We remained on the roof a while longer, watching the fires burn elsewhere in the city. The streets below were deserted now. A pall of smoke dampened the distant sounds of battle, still raging in the outskirts.

"It's time to bring the family back," Dad said, as the group broke up. "You two boys can go and tell them it's alright to come back now."

The thought of having been entrusted yet another grownup mission swelled us with pride. We had earned our place in the fraternity of men.

"Be careful with land mines," Dad called out as we ran down the stairs. "And make sure there are no Japs between here and the church." Just before reaching the main gate, on our way out, we heard one last admonition: "And don't tarry in between!"

He knew us well.

Avoiding the more exposed Calle Real, we snuck through the narrow alley leading to Plaza Libertad, and the San Jose church that dominated it. Sniffing around the corner of the alley to make sure the square was deserted, we dashed across the grass and ducked into the church.

The crowd inside was huddled in separate groups. Women knelt in the front pews, praying the Rosary out loud, while babies fidgeted and restless children scampered around the aisles. We found the family in the Baptistery, hunkering there like frightened rabbits, among the remains of the shattered baptismal font.

Our sudden arrival caused a stir among the refugees. The Baptistery was suddenly swarming with humanity, everyone wanting to hear news from the outside.

"How'd it go? Was anybody hurt? Did the house burn down?" asked Luis, in a tumble of questions.

"How's Dad? asked Mom anxiously, hugging us both in warm welcome. "Did you all manage to save the house? Everything must be alright, or you wouldn't be here!" she answered her own questions.

"Everything is O.K. It's all over," I said. "Dad said its O.K. for you to come home now."

"You're always bringing us good news! Thank God everything's alright!" For her, that was not just an idle expression of relief but a heartfelt prayer of thanksgiving. Her celestial advocacy probably had more to do with the house's survival than the fire brigade itself.

"Were there any Japs out there?" asked Luis.

"We didn't see any, coming here. We saw Uyeki, though, a moment ago. Hope he's gone to the front by now." We explained how Uyeki's platoon got raked by the P-39s.

"Holy cow!" exclaimed Luis. "I knew they were shooting up something. We saw them from the Baptistery window, as they flew past," he said, pointing at the window behind us. "We didn't tell Padre Jesus they were Air Cobras this time, though. Didn't want to upset him again, after they shot up his baptismal font last time," he giggled.

"Did you see Karmele when you came in?" whispered Pedro Mari Arana, nudging me knowingly. He knew how much I liked her. "She's in the church, somewhere!"

"Where?" I asked, turning around to scan the sea of faces crowding the Baptistery. I didn't see her right off but spotted her brother, Iñaki, standing by the door. I nodded at him in awkward greeting and approached him, hoping his sister would be nearby.

And then I saw her. She was standing right behind him, looking prettier than I remembered. And just as shy.

"Hi!" I greeted them, beaming mostly at her. Karmele's gray-green eyes smiled back, modestly. Even in the gathering dark, I could tell that she was blushing. Her light brown hair was done up in a pony tail, highlighting a long, graceful neck. She'd grown prettier, since I'd last seen her, months earlier, in that very church. But there was something different now. The fullness pushing against her sundress revealed the beguiling onset of womanhood. Girls sometimes do that overnight, in the tropics. The very thought set me aquiver.

"I'm glad you're back from that island, safe and sound," Karmele said, smiling her shy smile. "I heard all about it."

"It was exciting. I'll tell you all about it one of these days, when we got more time," I promised. "I've got to go now," I said, a little awkwardly. I hated leaving her so quickly, but the family was waiting to leave, and Iñaki was starting to frown suspiciously.

We were the only ones to leave the church. The rest decided to stay, rather than hazard the trip back to their homes just yet. Lawson and I led the group across the plaza, cautiously threading our way through the dark alley and home.

The reunion with the firefighting husbands and fathers was tearful and joyous. We sat on mattresses strewn around the basement floor, sharing stories about the day's incredible events. A certain lightness pervaded the group, despite the distant din of gunfire. There was a feeling that things couldn't get any worse, that relief was imminent. Even Mrs. Arana kept a lid on her dour oracles.

In the middle of supper, Eusebio stunned the group by announcing, matter-of-factly: "The roop of the Japanese storehouse across the street's on pire." The startling news struck me like one of our old fisherman friend's impromptu news reports.

"It's not real threatening," Eusebio added, reassuringly. "The wind's blowing the other way."

It had been rumored that the Japanese had hoarded foodstuff in the abandoned building. Lawson and I exchanged furtive glances across the dinner table. The exchanged winks signaled the course of action. "There's no point in letting all that good food go to waste," he seemed to be telling me, over his Mongo soup.

271

While the restless crowd milled around, wondering whether they'd left church too soon, Lawson and I slipped quietly out of the basement to have a look at the threatened building, standing less than twenty feet away from our main gate. The doomed structure, with flames now licking at its roof, reminded me of someone unaware that his hat was on fire.

Eusebio and Juan Sumalakay were equally intrigued. Before anyone noticed, all four of us had crossed the street, and were pushing on the padlocked door, trying to break in. When the lock finally yielded, we stumbled into a large storeroom. It was packed to the rafters with storage racks, sagging from the weight of merchandise. I noticed that the ceiling above us had started to catch on fire.

Running in and out of the maze of smoke-filled aisles, we searched through the racks, mouths watering in anticipation. I pulled down one box after another, frantically ripping the cardboard containers open, looking for canned food.

We found none. The boxes only contained an odd assortment of worthless office equipment and nondescript military issue. There were pencils and ping-pong balls, canvas belts and untold grosses of one-toed rubber shoes, the kind the Japanese used in jungle warfare; only the right-footed variety was in stock.

The silly grins of squelched enterprise gradually turned to giggles, until we were all laughing at our ridiculous predicament. The ceiling beams were now earnestly afire, small tongues of flame starting to drop on us. It was only a matter of time before the whole ceiling would collapse.

"*Mira dirâ!*" shouted Eusebio, above the crackling din of the overhead fire. He had just removed the lid of a large drum and was pointing excitedly at its contents. There were over a hundred bottles of different varieties of hard liquor inside, neatly stacked between layers of sawdust. Eusebio pulled out a bottle of gin, and with one deft stroke, smartly lopped its neck off against a wall. Taking a long swig, he offered the jagged bottle to Juan. They took turns sampling the long-forgotten fruits of toil.

The heat inside was unbearable. Lawson and I grabbed as many bottles as we could and left the burning storehouse. We made several more liquor runs after that, Luis and the Arana brothers joining us in the foray. Meanwhile, feeling little discomfort, the two servants had settled down to some heavy drinking.

With a smoldering mattress wrapped around them for protection against the raging fire, they sat in the middle of the storeroom floor, passing the jagged bottle around, in foggy camaraderie.

"Planting rice is never fun,
    Bent from morn till the set of sun..."

they sang the harvest song dissolutely, totally oblivious to the inferno swirling around them. The scene, at first, had a touch of hilarity about it, but I soon began to fear for their lives, when burning beams started crashing down around them.

Now in a drunken stupor, the two servants merely giggled when begged to leave. I finally gave up trying and dashed home to alert Dad. Bounding across the street into the

273

inferno, he dragged the inebriated servants out of the building. Eusebio was laughing insanely as he watched Juan Sumalakay double-dribbling a ping-pong ball out of the building, pretending it was a basketball.

After all the excitement, we settled down to a restless night in the basement. It had been two days since the landing, and there was still no sign of the Americans. We suspected the land mines were slowing them down. Though the dynamiting had ceased altogether, the sound of battle in the outskirts of town persisted unabated, the blush of tracers in the sky vying against the small light of the Milky Way.

Late that night, as the San Jose clock tower chimed midnight, Dad roused us all up.

"What's the matter?" asked several voices, sleepily.

"The Lizarraga building's on fire," he said darkly. "The wind's kicked up, and this time it's blowing our way."

The news sounded ominous; there were only a few houses standing between us and the Lizarraga's, to the north. Ours would not survive the night, if the wind kept its present drift. There was no alley or street barrier to save it, this time.

Everyone left for church, this time. Only Dad remained behind. Mom didn't say anything when she hugged him goodbye. She knew and understood his ingrained sense of duty and the done thing. He'd follow us only when all hope was lost, all honor exhausted. That was Dad. She couldn't change him now.

Except for the solitary candle burning near the altar, the San Jose church was dark and quiet when we got there. We could sense the humanity inside only from the repressed coughing and the occasional stirring of the crowd. Some other family had moved into the Baptistery after we'd left, earlier that afternoon, leaving us only the last few pews to lie down on. Someone nearby whispered anxious questions about the world outside, a baby cried, probably from hunger, but the church was, otherwise, quiet, hushed in fitful dreams.

It was a long, fretful night, filled with haunted dreams of burned homes and dashed hopes of early liberation. Even the thought of Karmele lying somewhere nearby held small solace. In the pew in front of me, I could hear Mom's rosary beads clicking softly against each other, throughout the night.

"You're gonna wake her up," I whispered to her, teasingly.

"Who? What?" she turned around, startled by my voice. She thought I was asleep.

"Your Virgin of Roncesvalles," I answered in a low voice. "She must be getting a headache from all those Hail Mary's you're sending her way."

"Hush," she whispered, scandalized by the remark. She always pretended shock at such impiety, a reaction which only goaded us to further teasing. It was a game we liked to play with her. "Go to sleep", she said, turning around.

Her beads clicked more softly now but she remained sitting up, eyes glued to the flickering lamp in the altar in front of her, lips moving in silent prayer. We were in good hands, I just knew.

24. LIBERATION

I'd been staring at the window above the choir all night, watching the moon's shinings and hidings in the unattached heavens. The first hint of dawn came when the stained glass window became gradually backlit by a diaphanous light. A cock crowed in Mari Kawayan's backyard nearby, confirming the imminence of dawn.

Dad had not turned up all night, boding either some misfortune or a relentless, single-handed combat with the fires. I had worried about his fate all night and was now determined to find out.

I could tell from the rhythmic wheezing and snoring sounds that the mass of humanity around me had finally succumbed to sleep. Even Mom was nodding now, in the pew in front of me. Quietly, I got up and tiptoed back to the front door of the church. Detecting no movement outside, I snuck out of the church and into Plaza Libertad.

Jumping in and out of foxholes, I dashed across the park until reaching the far end of the square. The shell of the burnt storehouse stood in front of me like a ghost, scratching

277

the dawning sky with gnarled, unforgiving fingers. I still couldn't see our house from where I stood, but the absence of a fire glow reassured me.

Sprinting across the street and through the debris-strewn alley, I emerged from the opposite end seconds later, to discover our house standing in the wandering smoke, unscathed. It was as though I were seeing it for the first time. Peering through the receding darkness, I distinguished Dad's figure, standing behind the wrought iron gate. Feet spread apart and arms akimbo, he seemed to be daring the world to wrest his home away from him.

Rushing to greet him, we embraced in silence. We'd been through a lot together those last twenty four hours, and now we just stood there, quietly celebrating life.

"What brings you here at this ungodly hour?" he asked.

"Just thought I'd check up on you," I responded, trying to sound grownup. "I was starting to worry."

"Well, as you can see, I'm still in one piece and the house still stands," he said, with the simple pride of achievement. "The wind shifted soon after you left. It's been quiet all night. Even the guerrillas seem to have wearied of shooting at the Japanese. It's all very strange. I feel like something's about to give."

He didn't use to share his thoughts with me like that before. A new camaraderie seemed to have sprung up between us overnight, and it filled me with a warm glow.

"Let's go up the street a-piece and look around," he proposed.

In the eerie quiet of dawn, we ambled up Calle de la Rama warily, heading toward the wharf. All that remained of the Lizarraga residence was a heap of smoldering rubble, puny tongues of flame licking at the smoke twirling out of the blackened timbers.

"I wonder if it couldn't have been saved," Dad commented, a note of sadness in his voice. It had been a grand Colonial home, like ours, but its owners had been away, in Manila, and its caretakers must have taken off at the first sign of danger.

Our footsteps resounded eerily in the deserted street as we headed back for home. There was an uncanny stillness all about, as dawn broke out resolutely over Guimarás. Even the birds seemed to be holding back their song, as animals sometimes do, just before an earthquake. The air was heavy with smoke, the morning so eagerly awaited, now heavy with uncertainty and foreboding.

"But where are the Americans?" I asked impatiently. "What's keeping them, anyway?"

"Surely, they're in the outskirts of town by now," said Dad. "Those land mines must have been more effective than I thought."

"Why is it so quiet, though?" I asked apprehensively. "It feels kind'a weird, doesn't it."

"Battles usually start at dawn," he answered distractedly. After mulling over what he had just said, he added: "I'd like for you to run over to church now and fetch the family. I'd like for all of us to be together again, whatever the outcome this time."

For the second time in less than twelve hours, I returned to church to convey Dad's message. It felt good to be the bearer of good tidings once again, but I was starting to feel like a broken record. They rejoiced at the news that Dad was alright and that the house still stood.

The excitement of homecoming soon receded into a disquieting silence. It was almost as if, reluctant to challenge it, we'd all agreed to mimic the stillness around us, keeping our own unacknowledged fears to ourselves. Breakfast was like a small wake. A faint I-told-you-so smirk wrinkled Mrs. Arana's lips. Thriving on tragedy, she seemed to sense the impending onset of her element. Her wry smile worried me even more.

I had just fished out the last weevil floating in my corn porridge when the first artillery shell slammed into something nearby. The thunderous explosion reverberated around the walls of the basement, rattling windowpanes and bouncing plates off the table. We stared at each other, mouths agape, pupils distended in terror.

"What was that?" asked several people in unison, spoons suspended halfway to their mouths. Before anyone could answer, pandemonium broke loose. Chairs screeched and people stumbled over each other as we all flew toward the air raid shelter. A mass of humanity piled into the cramped quarters. There must have been two dozen people shoehorned into an enclosure designed for no more than a dozen. Even Angel, the cook, and Sumalakay, the chauffeur, abandoned their erstwhile pretended nonchalance and joined the panicked melee.

The atmosphere inside was thick with fear. There was something terrifying about this new kind of bombardment; unlike airplane bombs, artillery shells were preceded by an eerie, high-pitched whistling sound. There was scarcely enough time for any mental steeling against the ensuing blast. Bursts simply occurred, each a spike of unguarded terror, exploding in the mind like a shriek from some avenging banshee, strewing thunderbolts about.

"*Ay, Señor San José*!" simpered Alíng Andáng in mortal fright. I watched her, chewing on her toothless gums between mumbled incantations, trembling in hysterical fear of death. In the small darkness, she reminded me of Millet's 'Man with the Hoe', in the lithograph that used to hang from our classroom wall, a face untouched by anything remotely akin to conceptual thought. But, unlike the depicted brute, Alíng could grieve and die many small deaths of terror, as she was doing right there, in front of me. Besides, I thought, this one knew how to pray.

The blasts grew louder. I sensed with mounting concern that the gunnery officer wasn't just shooting for effect, the way he was marching his shells down Calle Real toward home, deliberately correcting his aim after every shot. The approaching barrage struck terror in everyone's heart as the shells burst ever closer.

Oblivious to the paroxysm around him, Angelito, the cook's four year-old son, started pestering Pedro Mari Arana, sidling up closer to him and generally making a nuisance of himself. Trying to discourage him, Pedro Mari suddenly cut loose with a silent exhalation of green-foul wind.

"*Ay abaw, ka bahû!*" howled the child, scrambling to bury his offended nostrils in the folds of his mother's sarong. With deadly pervasiveness, the fetid cloud drifted slowly across the enclosure, raising blisters of indignation as it floated obnoxiously by. Pedro Mari's and my howls of laughter broke the oppressive tension in the shelter. Everyone, except Pedro Mari's mother, joined in the nervous laughter.

"Hey, the shelling's stopped!" announced Lawson, soon after the laughter had died down. He was always the first to notice things like that.

A sudden hush fell over the group as we strained to listen to the prolonged silence, interrupted only by Aling's nervous gumming. People soon started stirring restlessly. We'd been sitting in the cramped quarters for several hours and it was time to stretch and breathe some fresh air. One by one we stood up, ducking warily out of the shelter and into the blinding light of day. For the first time since Guimarás, I smelled the subtle, indefinable smell of sunlight on green leaves, and I knew that it was good to be free and alive again.

We were still milling around the downstairs patio half an hour later, when Iñaki Elordi turned up, panting and out of breath. He had run all the way from home to share a strange and wonderful tale.

"The nuns at the Sagrado Corazon did it!" he said breathlessly. "The Japs told them they were leaving town, so the nuns told the Americans to stop the shelling. And they did!"

"You're barmy!" replied Lawson, offended at the thought of his nuns deigning to even talk to the Japanese. "What are you gibbering about? You're making no sense at all! Get a grip on!"

"Didn't you see that small Piper Cub airplane circling over town while all the shelling was going on?" persisted Iñaki.

"Yeah, we saw it." We hadn't, of course, but we weren't about to let Iñaki one-up us on anything. We still couldn't figure out what the nuns had to do with it.

"Well, Dad says it was an artillery spotter plane," Iñaki held forth, volubly. "The nuns went out on the beach and wrote a message on the sand, using white stones, reading: 'NO JAPS IN CITY.' And guess what? The pilot swooped down on them and dropped a wrench nearby, with a note attached to it that said: "We got the message and told Headquarters; signed The Navy". That's all it said".

He paused for effect. "And then the shelling stopped!"

"I knew it!" exclaimed Lawson, surprised and touched by the news. "Those little nuns saved our lives; mine, for the second time!"

It had been a stroke of good fortune. We later learned that the Japanese Colonel, who had billeted in the Shrubsole's bungalow near the Convent, had befriended the nuns and told them, the night before, that they were pulling out of town and were heading for the hills.

"Cutting through guerrilla lines," he had confided to Sor Felicidad, "will be easier than facing the Americans."

Unaware that they'd been given the slip, the Americans, meanwhile, were getting ready to soften up the enemy - and us - before proceeding with the final assault. Their intention had been to level the town rather than reenact the bloody house-to-house combat they'd just experienced in Manila, only a month earlier.

"We probably would have all perished in the rubble, hadn't it been for those little nuns," said Dad, realizing the close call. "I can just see that spotter pilot looking down on them and puzzling over the message they were writing on the sand."

"We should remember to thank the nuns for saving our lives with their quick thinking," proposed Mom.

There was a brief lull after Iñaki left, when nothing seemed to be happening. We just stood around in separate groups, as if nervously awaiting the Second Coming. Slowly, people began to emerge from their homes, milling around the sidewalks aimlessly, like souls straying out of purgatory, dazed by the sweet, forgotten taste of freedom.

"It took McArthur a while, but he finally returned," gushed a disbeliever.

"As promised!" responded another, voicing his mixed feelings of joy and disbelief at the sudden happy ending of nightmare.

It was midday before we saw the first Americans. Several jeeps carrying engineers from a Bomb Disposal squad were riding point for the 40th Division's main force. Careening deftly around the mines on the street, one of them stopped almost directly in front of me. Several soldiers hopped out of the vehicle, rifles at the ready, looking around warily for snipers.

"Hi, there!" I hailed the tall redheaded Corporal who was looking quizzically at me. "There aren't any Japs around, if that's what you're looking for," I volunteered, trying to be helpful.

"Yeah!" confirmed others around me. "They skipped town last night!"

The redhead wasn't taking anybody's word for it. He was all business. He ordered the milling crowd to stand back while his buddies defused the mines on the street. After talking into his Walkie Talkie, he hopped back into his jeep and proceeded down the street.

The first Sherman tanks clanked into view shortly after, brimming with soldiers. Half a dozen infantrymen were riding on top of each behemoth, hunkering on track guards and hanging onto gun turrets, waving back at the crowd.

"Hi Joe!" cheered the enraptured mob. Women in balconies and windows tossed flowers and blew kisses at the grimy warriors. Others on the street rushed out to hug and kiss the bemused soldiers. There was unabashed adulation for the blond strapping giants ambling down both sides of the street with easy, athletic stride, their young, sunny faces and ready smiles a striking contrast to the dour scowls of their predecessors.

The transition was electric. An almost tangible sense of relief and gratitude gushed from the crowd, euphoric with survival. It was like emerging from a harrowing night into a morning alive with sunshine, surfacing from despair to jubilation. I consciously tucked those moments away in some nook of memory because I sensed that the likes of them would never be again.

I rushed upstairs to watch the triumphal entry from a better vantage point from the living room windows. The rest of the family was caught up in the frenzy, waving at the marching soldiers. The young warriors looked up, surprised to see Europeans, and started lobbing cans of Spam and chocolate bars into our windows. Memories of Antonio and his K-Rations came flooding back. Picking up several bottles of gin and whisky from the previous night's raid, I tossed them down to our liberators. They laughed at the unexpected exchange of gifts.

The soldiers paraded in and out of our house all afternoon, making short shrift of our supply of salvaged liquor. It seemed, at times, as if a whole regiment had dropped in for a social visit. There was something innocent and noble about these gentle warriors. Generous to a fault, they plied us with food and forgotten luxuries.

"Can I hold your carbine?" asked Lawson of one of the soldiers sitting in the kitchen table, trying to make conversation with the young Arana maid. He looked at Lawson, puzzled more by his freckles and sandy hair than by his odd request.

"O.K." he answered reluctantly. "But don't drop it," he added, handing him the rifle, after making sure the safety lock was on.

Lawson picked up the weapon almost reverently, first caressing its stock and then passing his hand gently over the barrel, like a blind man feeling a woman's face. Raising the weapon to his shoulder, he took careful aim at an imaginary target outside the kitchen porch and curled his finger around the trigger.

"Boom!" he whispered almost inaudibly. I could just see his thoughts flashing back to the cave tucked away behind the waterfall. We would remember that evening for the rest of our lives.

"I wonder where that perishing beggar Uyeki is now," Lawson asked no one in particular, putting the gun down where it had been propped.

"Who?" asked the soldier who had been watching Lawson's curious shooting ritual with keen interest.

"Oh, nothing," answered the Scot, laconically. "Just some Jap."

I hadn't thought about it all those years but I suddenly realized that Lawson had more reason than I to despise the Japanese; I had only lost two dogs to them, he had lost his parents.

"They took off for the hills," said the American. "You were lucky." It was then we learned about the massacre in Manila, a month earlier.

"No," he said, in answer to Lawson's query about Santo Tomás. "We managed to get to the concentration camp before they could kill 'em all. That was their plan, you know. Those internees were in pretty sad shape."

25. EPILOGUE

Life limped back to normal, but only falteringly. People trickled down from the hills, dazed by the ruin about them. Running water and electricity were restored soon enough, but everything else remained shattered, almost as if the land's topsoil had been blown away, gone the way of the 'Co-Prosperity Sphere,' which the Japanese had so boringly touted. San Agustin took its sweet time reopening. The damage sustained from the bombing that Lawson and I had witnessed from the heights of Guimarás, had to be repaired. Having had school breaks before, we took the latest one in happy stride.

We met many American Officers during the few weeks the Fortieth Division remained in town. They'd drop in for drinks, evenings, and sometimes stayed for supper. It was almost like old times. Mom, ever the gracious hostess, managed to breathe one last breath of life into the long-dead Belle Époque. Though still uncomfortable with his English, Dad humored her and went along with the soirees and candlelit dinners she'd organize.

A young Navy Lieutenant came in from the rain, one evening. His bearded smile gave him less the air of a warrior than a poet, which, it turned out, he was.

"Hi," he said, with a faint Tennessee drawl. "My name's Jac Chambliss." His blue eyes twinkled as he explained that his ship had just put into port that morning, and that a friend had told him about us. There was a certain grace of motion and unstudied sensitivity about him that belied the inner toughness of an ex Golden Gloves boxer and a feisty lawyer.

Jac struck a resonant chord with Mom when he recognized her hometown's name. "Burguete! Why, that's the town in the Pyrenees where Hemingway went fishing and wrote about in "The Sun Also Rises!" Mom, of course, knew.

Jac offered to send a telegram to my grandmother in Burguete, to let her know we were alive and well. We later learned that Grandmother had summoned the town doctor to translate it. That was fortunate because she fainted right there, in front of him, from the excitement of learning about our survival. She had given us up for dead, after news of the Manila massacre.

Jac became a regular dinner guest during his ship's stay in port. He'd turn up with a freshly baked loaf of bread, which we'd devour ravenously, not having had any in years. Mom would serve him Spam, believing it to be some gourmet delicacy. She was puzzled when he'd turn it down, asking, instead, for a second helping of Mongo soup. We all found that quite amusing.

"Who made this model airplane?" he asked one day, picking up the P-38 I'd carved during the occupation. "It's pretty good!"

"I did," I answered proudly, pleased with the compliment. "Copied it from a picture in an old magazine. I've never seen one up close, though" I explained, hoping Jac could arrange for me to see one.

"Well, I think we can do something about that," Jac said with a smile. In a borrowed jeep, he drove Luis, Lawson and me the Jaro airfield, the next day. There were no P-38's around but, there, sitting darkly on the tarmac, was a P-61 night fighter. The airplane lacked the slick grace of the Lightning, but both warplanes were strikingly similar, both with their three-body configuration.

"They call this the Black Widow," Jac explained. "It's the first warplane to use radar."

"What's that?" I asked.

"It's some electronic devise on its nose that allows the pilot to see at night. I think that's why they call it the 'Black Widow'; it makes a lot of Jap widows when their husbands are shot down in night combat."

I was impressed. "Could we take a look at it? Close up, I mean?"

Jac asked the pilot if he'd let us look around inside the new fighter. He agreed.

I was up first in the cockpit. There was a smell of new leather and gasoline inside. The instrument panel spread out before me with a boggling variety of knobs and dials and toggle switches. Settling down in the pilot's seat, I reached over and grabbed the joystick, yanking it hard towards me, pretending I was pulling a high acceleration maneuver to shake off an imaginary Zero tailing me.

The pilot, who was standing on the tarmac below, blanched.

"Hey," he bellowed up the stairwell, in panic. "Don't touch that stick!"

He'd forgotten that the machine guns had been armed for that night's strafing mission. The little red button on top of the joystick I was jerking around would have fired the weapons, if depressed. The guns' dark snouts were pointed directly at Luis, who was at that moment clambering up the ladder to join me in the cockpit. I gasped, realizing I could have sliced him in half!

We were unceremoniously hustled out of the plane and driven back home, chastened. Lawson didn't even get to see the inside of the cockpit.

The Americans set up camp wherever they could. The Bomb Disposal squad that had cleared the land mines on liberation day settled in the basement of Campos' knick-knack shop, just across the street from us. Intrigued by the odd lot of human flotsam huddling there, Lawson, Luis and I would visit the motley crew practically every day,

Of the desperadoes, 'Injun Joe' was, by far, the most peculiar. Certifiably insane, the burly, half-breed Navaho would jump up from his cot and head for the small restroom in the back, ululating war-whoops as he un-holstered his .45. There, he'd proceed to blaze away at the toilet bowl and its now-orphaned commode. The roar was deafening. Seconds later, the redheaded Indian loomed out of the smoke, a beatific grin on his face. His equally unstable buddies had remained in their cots, reading their comics as if nothing had happened. No one complained about their savaged facilities.

Despite the occasional mayhem, the Bomb Disposal loonies taught us some useful lessons. One of them was to never tamper with mortar fuses or hand grenades. Injun Joe drooled as he showed us inert samples of both, explaining their inner workings in his garbled Bronx accent.

It wasn't more than a week later that Iñaki Elordi discovered a Japanese cache of mortar fuses in the beach where Lawson and I had once landed with the Sea Hawk, in brazen but unfulfilled challenge to the Rising Sun. Iñaki had picked up several mortar fuses and taken them home with him, unaware that the dampness from exposure to the elements had only temporarily duded them. Their detonators soon dried out, however, and, one day, trying to prove their inertness to us, Iñaki set off one of the fuses, blowing half the fingers in one hand away. No one else was seriously hurt, but Luis still occasionally picks tiny slivers of shrapnel from one of his arms, half a century later.

Several weeks after the landing, the Americans were still fighting the Japanese, who had managed to slip through the guerrilla noose, and holed up in the hills to fight another day. The Japanese put up a stiff resistance, fighting to the bitter end. Even so, a few reluctant survivors emerged from the fray.

Looking out of the living room window one afternoon, Lawson and I saw a convoy of 6x6 trucks rumbling past. A group of captured Japanese soldiers sat stiffly upright on the benches of the uncovered vehicles, staring morosely at each other across the aisle. People in the street stopped to ogle the prisoners. But their initial surprise soon turned ugly and they started hurling insults and stones at the passing convoy.

Suddenly, I saw him. There, sitting on a truck facing us, was Uyeki himself! He had been looking up at me as his truck approached, baleful eyes peering behind round, wire-rimmed glasses that glinted briefly in the sun. Twice in as many months, our gazes had met in a mutual exchange of loathing. Before he rode past earshot, I pointed at Lawson with a crooked thumb, and shouted out to him:

"Watakushi no otooto desu!"

His eyes narrowed to a slit, his lips faintly curling into a malignant smirk, still disbelieving my claiming Lawson as a brother.

"I-i-e-e!" he bellowed in furious and unrepressed denial. His voice shattered the afternoon quiet, growing fainter as the truck rumbled off into the distance.

"What was that all about?" asked Lawson, intrigued by the interchange.

"He still doesn't believe you're my brother!"

We both burst out laughing.

"That sour smile on the rotter's face was worth three years of hell!"

"You betcha!"

Someone told us, a week later, that Uyeki had been summarily executed. A military court had found him guilty of murdering a young boy for drawing a Lightning shooting down a Zero, on a building wall. The boy had survived the brutal mauling sustained while hanging in a suspended sack. But when they took him down, Uyeki had finished him off with a shot in the head from his .45.

I was shocked by the news. My thoughts hurtled back to years of innocence, when Uyeki had played the harmonica in front of the class and had helped us solve math problems on his abacus. He had tried to straddle two worlds and ended up losing both.

After supper that evening, I got out an old Geography book from a stack of old textbooks I kept under my bed. "I want to show you something," I said to Lawson, opening the large blue book to its first page. There, spilling over the Ex Libris glued to the front page, was my name, written with baroque flourish.

"Uyeki wrote this, many years ago," I said.

Lawson made as if to pass his fingers over the weathered handwriting on the time-mottled page. Checking his hand in midair, he quickly brought it back down to his side, as if catching himself midstride, just in time to avoid treading on unhallowed ground.

Shortly after the American army finally left Panay en route to Japan, a portly, linen-suited Englishman blew into town. He was the Far Eastern representative of the British-owned Hongkong & Shanghai National Bank, then headquartered in Bangkok. He'd been sent to reopen his bank's Iloilo branch office. Since all the hotels in town had been leveled, Dad invited Mr. Waite to stay with us.

Mr. Waite and Lawson didn't hit it off, from the start; the chemistry just wasn't there. That surprised me a little, considering their shared allegiance to the same British Crown.

"He's such a Colonel Blimp!" muttered Lawson enigmatically.

"What do you mean?" I asked, puzzled.

"He's so ruddy English!" commented the irritated Scot. "Just listen to him!"

I soon grasped the nuance of 'blimp-ness'. Our gimlet-eyed guest was full of pat little phrases which he'd spew out through unmoving lips, in a clipped, self-conscious sort of way. The way he'd start each sentence with 'actually,' was starting to irritate me. I soon also wearied of his puckish hyperbole. Things weren't just 'awful'; they had to be 'perfectly ghastly'. Things were either a sporting 'jolly good show!' or a 'frightful sort of rot, what?' I started to suspect that Colonel Blimp must have been a ridiculous man.

Mr. Waite came back from his first inspection tour of the bank, muttering something about 'those dastardly Jap chaps!' for making such a 'frightful shambles' of his offices.

"All those checks lying about like a ghastly ticker tape parade!" he complained in upper-crusty indignation, aquiline nose sniffing the air as if someone in the room had passed wind. Lawson and I exchanged furtive glances. If he'd only known the wonder and delight of that magnificent battle royal!

"Could I bother you for some stationary?" he asked at breakfast the next morning. "I have a report to write and I'm afraid I've misplaced my tablet in Bangkok, with the rush and all that sort of thing, what?"

"Got it," volunteered Lawson without hesitation. Getting up from the table, he headed straight for the box of 'goodies' he kept under his bed. After rummaging through it, he came up with several crisp bond paper sheets and handed them over to Mr. Waite. I braced myself; the Cheshire cat smile on Lawson's face boded mischief.

"Absolutely spiffing, what?" said the delighted Englishman, taking the sheets. Suddenly, his eyes focused on the letterhead; there, prominently displayed at the top of the page, was the name of his very own Bank! He gawked at the sheets in front of him, pupils distended, jaw dropping in a graceless, jowly gape. I gulped, wondering what had gotten into Lawson to turn in State's evidence that readily.

"Where on earth did you come by this stationary?" Mr. Waite demanded gruffly, fairly losing his composure. I couldn't wait for the 'denouement', as Jesus Jimenez liked to call tight little scrapes like this.

"Oh, we found them strewn about," answered Lawson with the serenity of a jackhammer. "We figured we'd save them for some special occasion like this." He paused for effect. "Good thinking, wouldn't you say?" he added with deadpan expression.

"Rawtha!" declared Mr. Waite, still perplexed. Lawson had not even cracked a smile throughout the improbable explanation. 'Nice gambit, Davies!' I thought to myself, relieved but still looking down at my hands on the table, afraid to look him in the eye for fear we'd both crack up.

"I wonder if he fell for that cock-and-bull story of yours," I later remarked to Lawson.

"It's not how you play the game," sniggered Lawson. "It's whether you win that counts."

His logic, somehow, didn't ring quite true. An odd Mediterranean twist had now been added to the original British sense of fairplay. Lawson had been away from his roots too long. He would have to be reprogrammed when he returned home.

We never figured out whether Mr. Waite's ensuing coolness was to compensate for his having lost it during the little inquisition, or because of a growing suspicion that he'd been bested by the picaresque young Scot. He left town shortly after with a limp upper lip and his pecker definitely down.

Several weeks after the Blimp interlude, we saw a movie called Brigadoon, where grownup men could be seen running around the Scottish moors in plaid skirts, bashing each other lustily with enormous broadswords. That night in bed, Lawson said: "I'd love to see my brothers again."

Ever since the liberation, he'd been mentioning Scotland with growing insistence. The knowledge that he would leave us one day had always been there, just below the surface of conscious thought. It seemed inevitable. I sensed that the time was drawing near when there would be a parting of the ways, he to his moors, I to my Basque highlands.

Before returning to Bangkok, Mr. Waite had contacted the British Legation in Manila and alerted them to Lawson's whereabouts. He'd also asked them to track down Lawson's family in Scotland to let them know that he had survived the war.

A month passed before Lawson heard from the Legation. Passage had been arranged for him on a military transport plane leaving for Manila the following week. There, he would join a group of British ex-internees, and board a P. & O. liner for their trip back to England. His oldest brother, now an engineer, had married and would be waiting for him in London to take him to their home, in Aberdeen.

Though delighted with the news, Lawson tried to smother his excitement so as not to appear insensitive to our sadness at his imminent departure. Preparations were made for his trip. Mom stayed up late, nights, knitting woolen sweaters and socks for him.

"I know how cold it gets where you're going. I don't want you catching a death of cold after surviving three and a half years of war," she said, with motherly concern.

Engrossed in a blur of clicking needles, I watched her lips moving in silent prayer, an occasional tear rolling down her cheeks. Only then did I realize that she was about to lose a son.

"I'll miss you when you're gone," I told him in a choked whisper, the last night we were together. It was like pushing a hesitant door open that should have remained shut. Sharp as a dart, the poignant moment hurt something inside me, pricking it with a strange and sudden loneliness. We'd gone through a lot together and the bonding from all those years of shared joy and peril would not be easily unraveled. We had been, and would remain, brothers.

"So will I," he answered with equal feeling. There was an awkward silence as our small words wandered out in the dark, leaving our inmost thoughts unuttered, like birds that once sang and were now still.

"Probably we'll see a lot of each other when we're both back in Europe," he added, hopefully. "It's not that big, you know."

Juan Sumalakay drove us to the airport in the ancient Ford the next day. The diminutive chauffeur sat stiffly upright in the driver's seat, feet barely reaching the pedals. Dad and we three boys were squinched up in the cab, next to him. We said little during the short trip, each one wrapped in his own thoughts of parting.

We stood around in a circle on the tarmac, bidding our last farewells while the engines of the guppy-shaped C-47 airplane roared impatiently nearby.

"I don't know how to say this," said Lawson awkwardly, eyes magnified by brimming tears. He looked at Dad, and said: "I was born to my parents. They were kind'a stuck with me. But you *chose* me." They embraced, and then he added: "Thank you." That was all he could say.

We hugged, inarticulately, and then he was gone.

Months would pass before we heard from him. His trip to England had taken a long time but he made it there, safely.

"The moors are pretty, as I knew they'd be," he wrote in his first letter. "And so are the lassies!" That made me envious.

His closing sentence moved me.

"Someday," he wrote, "when we're really grown up, let's both go back and visit Nalunga and Nadulao. Just for Auld Lang Syne."

But, unlike the famous warrior who returned after leaving them in some haste, I have not been back to those enchanted isles again, afraid their magic spell would snap. Only dreams transport me now to haunting shores of long ago, to child-man years, charmed even more by time and space.